NELL

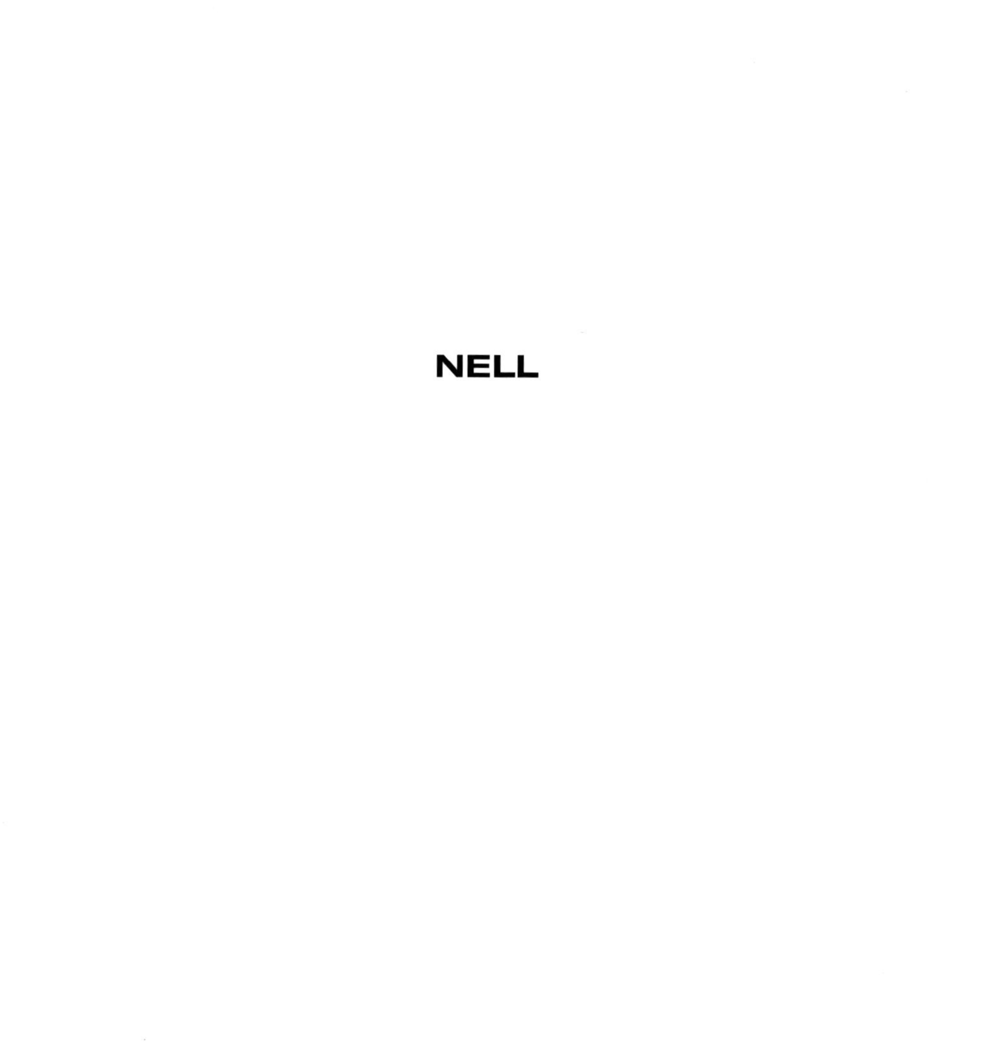

NELL

Series Editor Natalie King

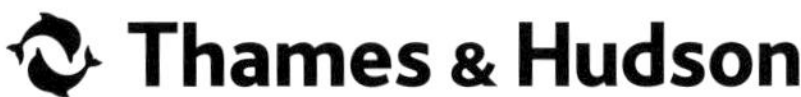

SKETCHES OF PLEASURE AND PAIN

ROBERT FORSTER

I have been to the University of Queensland Art Museum building before, then it was called Mayne Hall, and I did exams there in the late seventies as a student. Concerts were also held in the hall, and in 1979, I saw Tom Waits perform with a small band. It was a good concert – the strongest memory of the night, however, does not involve music: between songs, someone yelled out something stupid to the stage. The long, embarrassed silence that fell on the audience, finally punctured by Waits's raspy drawl, 'Yeah… I remember my first beer too.'

Forty years later, viewing a number of Nell's paintings from her series *Blessings* at the UQ Art Museum, featuring no-nonsense one liners, 'you made my SHIT LIST', connected to a dark-humoured image, a smiling piece of shit, I cannot help but wonder what image Nell would attach to such suitable subject matter as the long-ago Waits riposte.

I had first encountered Nell's work when I was invited to be interviewed at the Gold Coast City Gallery's *Primavera at 25* exhibition in July 2017. There, I met Nell and had the pleasure of seeing – experiencing is a better word – the overwhelming beauty and ecstatic shimmer of *Unlimited Radiance*. I liked the title too, and I was quick to learn when viewing more of her art that words – their twisting, their power, the possibilities inherent in their design – are of great importance to Nell; an essential ingredient to her varied artistic practice.

Two years later, on August 7, 2019, I am visiting the UQ Art Museum to see the *Blessings* paintings in a group exhibition entitled *Workshop*. I had come to the museum to write on Nell's work, noting my good fortune in being able to view recent work of hers in my hometown. My intention, to experience the work in its context, and to assemble my thoughts and impressions later when writing this essay. But this doesn't happen; my careful plan ambushed by the exhibition itself.

The museum had taken the title of the exhibition literally; the art, bordered off by crude wooden panelling to suggest a 'workshop'; amidst the art, a workbench with art supplies – coloured pens, pencils, paper – and on wooden racks near the bench are stacked art books and magazines. With these tools before me, and accepting the connection being made between the art of the artist and the experience and potential art of the viewer, I take a pencil and sheet of paper. My response to Nell's art will not be as contemplative as I'd imagined, but more spontaneous – a sketch if you like, as I circle the work.

There are twelve paintings before me, each roughly a metre high and half a metre wide, laid out in rows, four across and three down, against a white wall. This creates a mosaic effect, allowing visual and textural themes to blend in the process, creating a unity of intent and second visual punch when standing at a distance back from the art, which I do. Some figurative characteristics of the paintings are immediately evident too – the mix between text-laden work or word-work and those with a strong single image – the empty-eyed, open-mouthed jellyfish and egg-shaped images peering out from the canvases that stand in contrast to the one other face, the smiling piece of shit. Who is, or are, this person or people or presences? A room full of them, disembodied heads on stools, appear in an earlier work, *The Wake*. Their features too minimally delineated to suggest gender, they are vessels perhaps, faces of the artist or her consciousness, astonished, appalled, amused at what they see.

Taken together, the paintings have a simplicity to their appearance, prodding you to establish connections and meaning: opposing and complementing ideas give the boxed grid of paintings a playful tension. Vulnerability and toughness coexist: 'LEAVE ME ALONE YOU FUCK', screams a spooked open mouth. Beside it, in gorgeous warm blue, black and orange tones, is the sentence 'I can see the LIGHT of a Clear BLUE morning'. 'I LIGHT BLUE' when read in capitals. The swings between doubt/faith, darkness/light, sadness/forever joy are listed within *prayer for MOTHER EARTH*. The clearest expression of this duality, and a warm yet tough humour that runs through her art, is found in *DOWN to YOU is UP*: a white arrow on a black background points up to DOWN, a black arrow on white background points down to UP. Simple. The title references a line from 'Pale Blue Eyes' by the sixties New York rock group The Velvet Underground; it's their gentlest song, from a band who can howl in ear-shattering feedback.

Rock 'n' roll and spiritual practice are interlocking constants; in *QUIET/LOUD*, Nell sits in meditation on a Marshall guitar amp, the last two letters absent from the maker's name emblazoned across the speaker cabinet. Dropped off? Chipped off? Or a deliberate feminisation of this most iconic of hard rock amps to read Marsha? Another work concerning the loud and mighty is the clever transforming of a song title, from Melbourne rock band The Birthday Party, into a beautiful 'religious-themed' piece: six guitar strings twined with red crystal beads form a crown of thorns titled *The Six Strings That Drew Blood*. Surprisingly, the rock band most referenced in Nell's thoughtful, feminised, Buddhist-inspired artistic practice is AC/DC (seventies slang for bisexuality). The group's distinctive band iconography adorns a black-robed, headless mannequin surrounded by plain Christian crosses, providing a riot of meaning in *Let There Be Robe*, a wordplay on the AC/DC hit 'Let There Be Rock'. You could say rock music and its culture is in her work in spirit; a last look at the twelve paintings as I leave *Workshop* confirms this; their boldness and directness and humour and questing spirituality, found in the best rock 'n' roll.

The last work of Nell's I see is on the lawn in front of the museum. Titled, appropriately, *Happy Ending*, and in proximity to a group of students lounging in deckchairs; it's a rounded headstone sitting crooked into the ground as they are in old church graveyards, cut into the headstone are two empty eyes and a curved smile. Joy in death. Making life light.

I drive home.

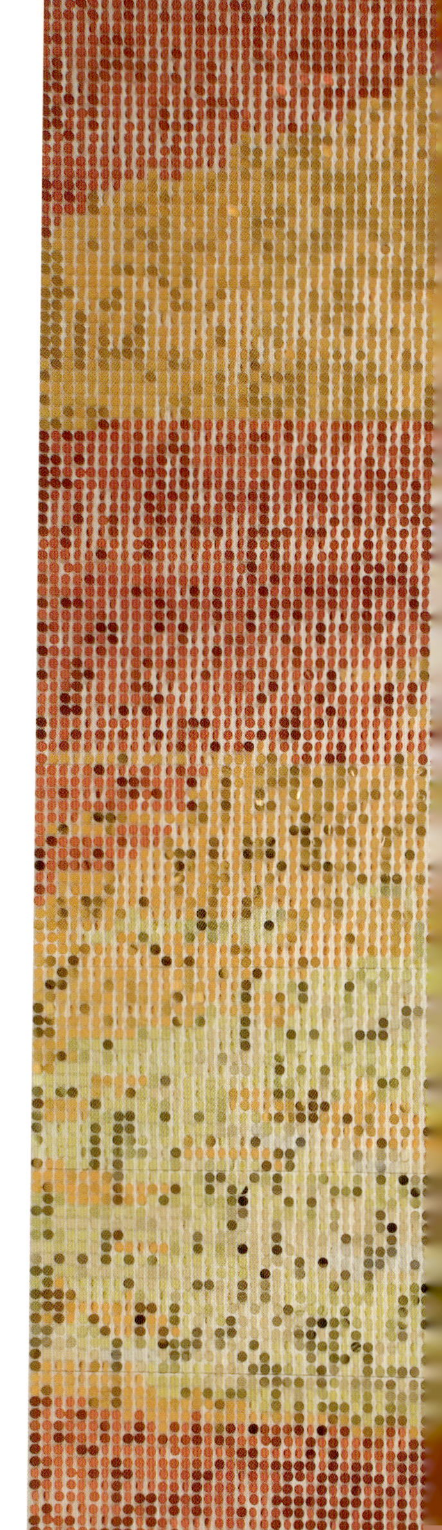

Unlimited Radiance
2001

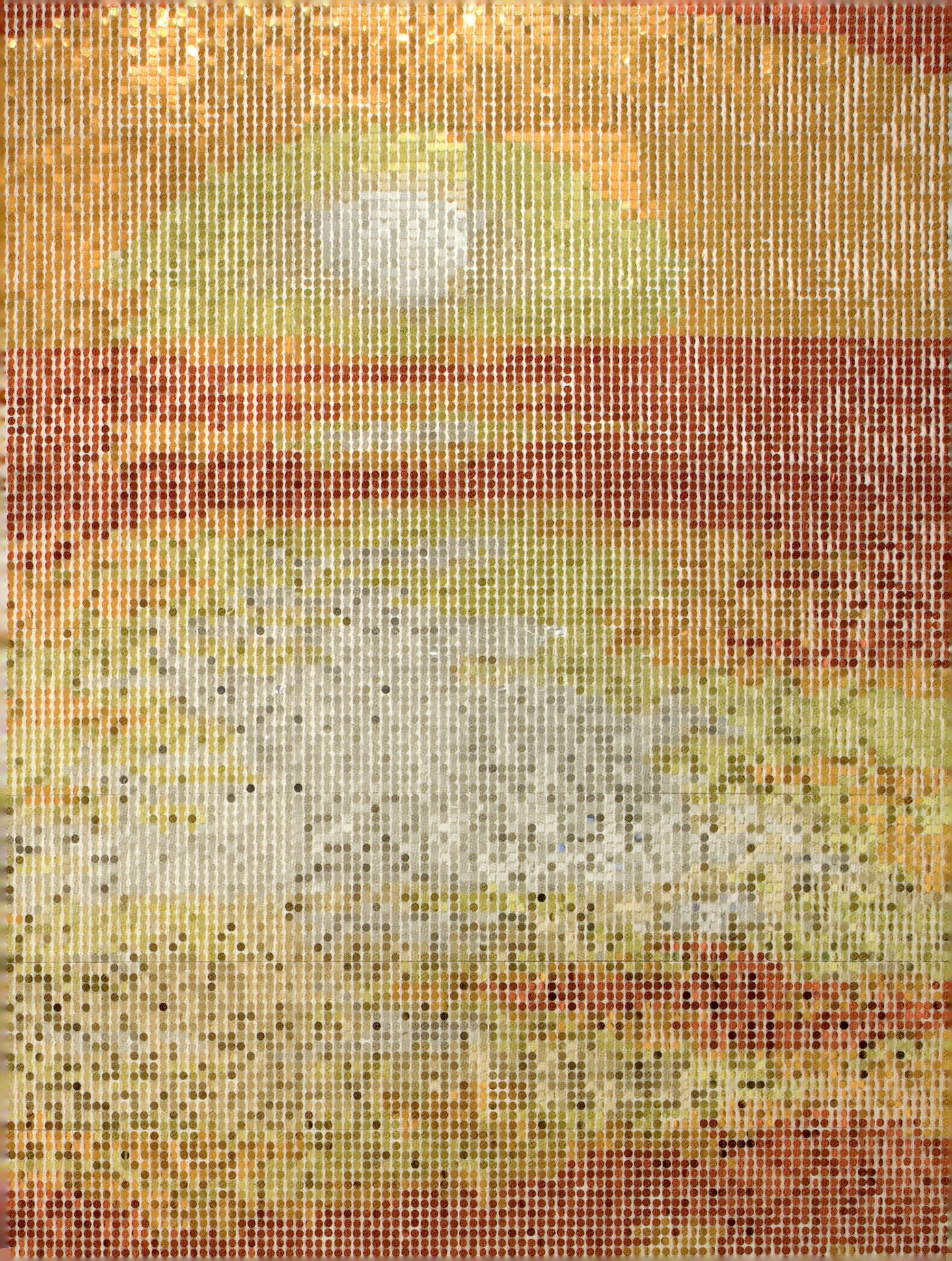

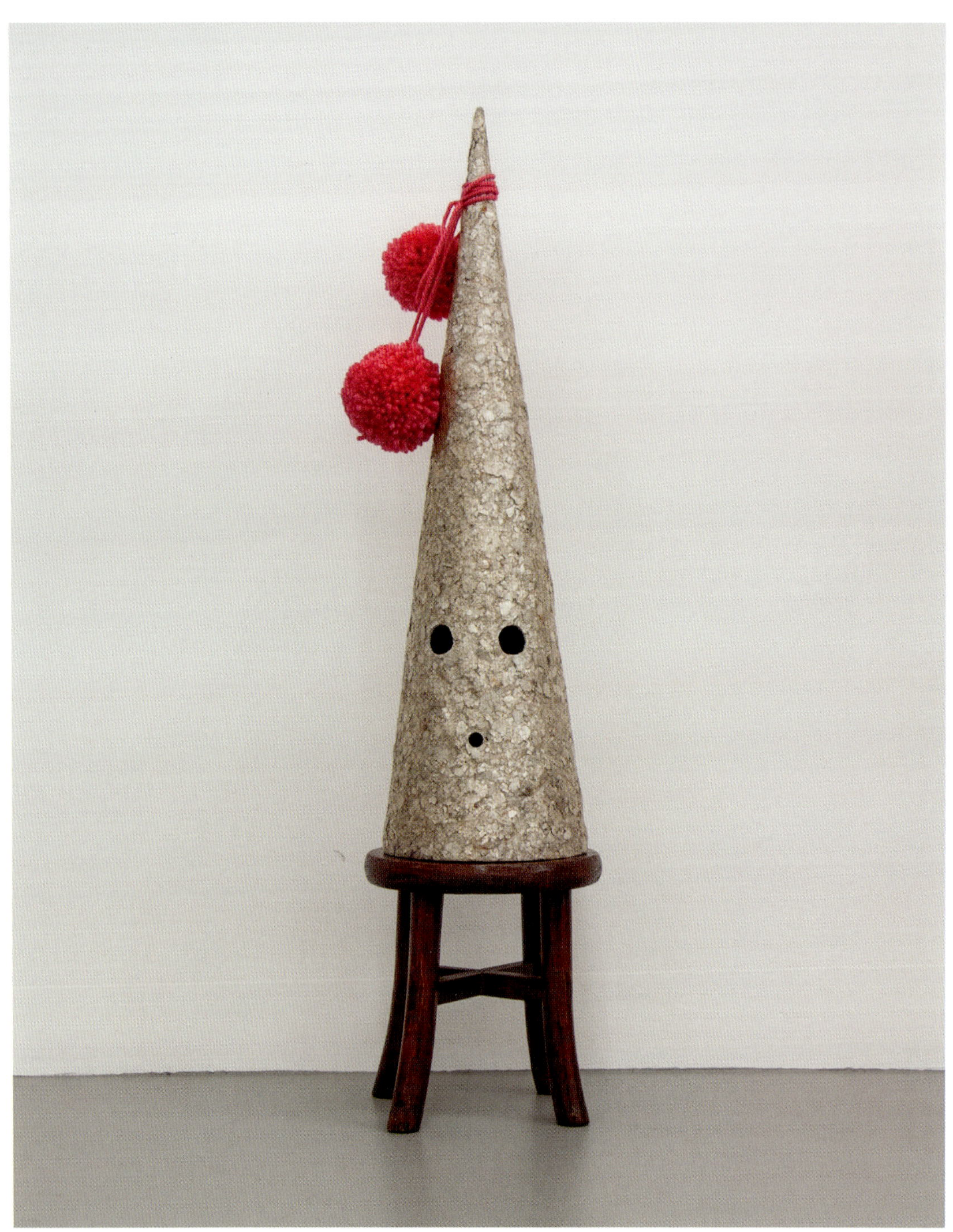

ooh
2016

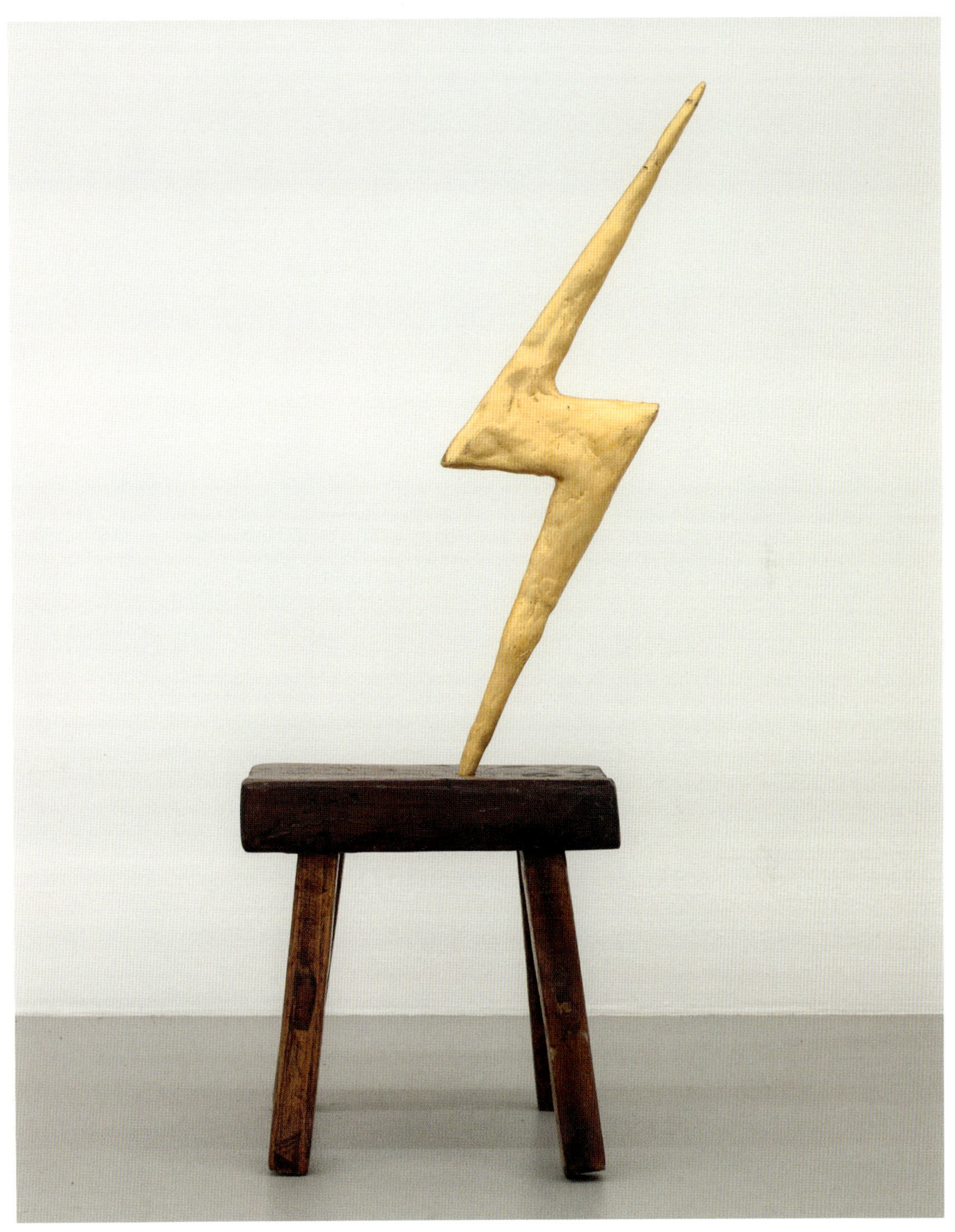

Who Made Who/One on One
2004–13

the WORLD fleeting

a ★ @ dawn

a bubble on a stream

a flash of lightning in a SUMMER

A flickering LAMP

a PHANTOM

a DREAM... ...

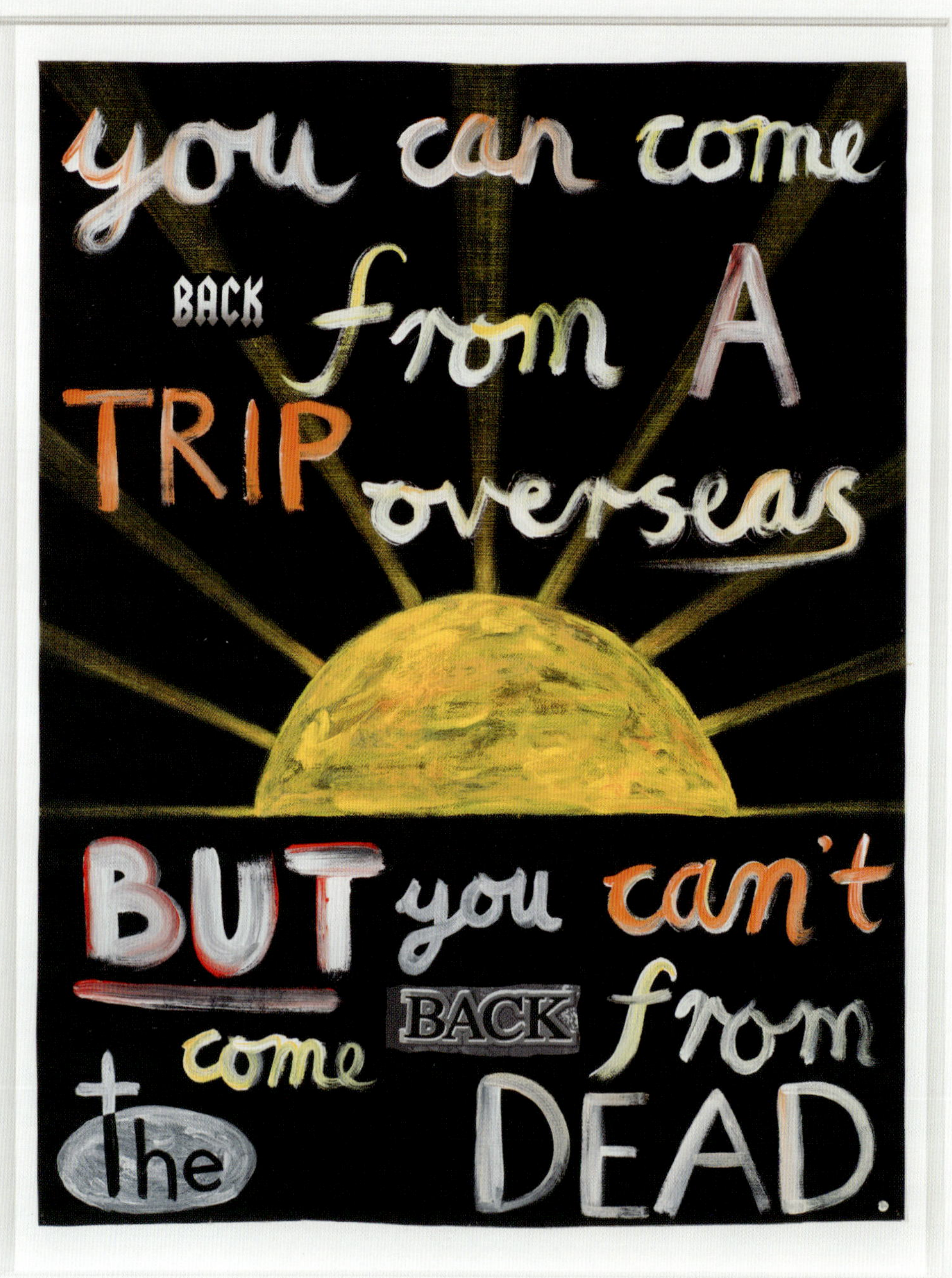

Not just an Australian Problem
2018

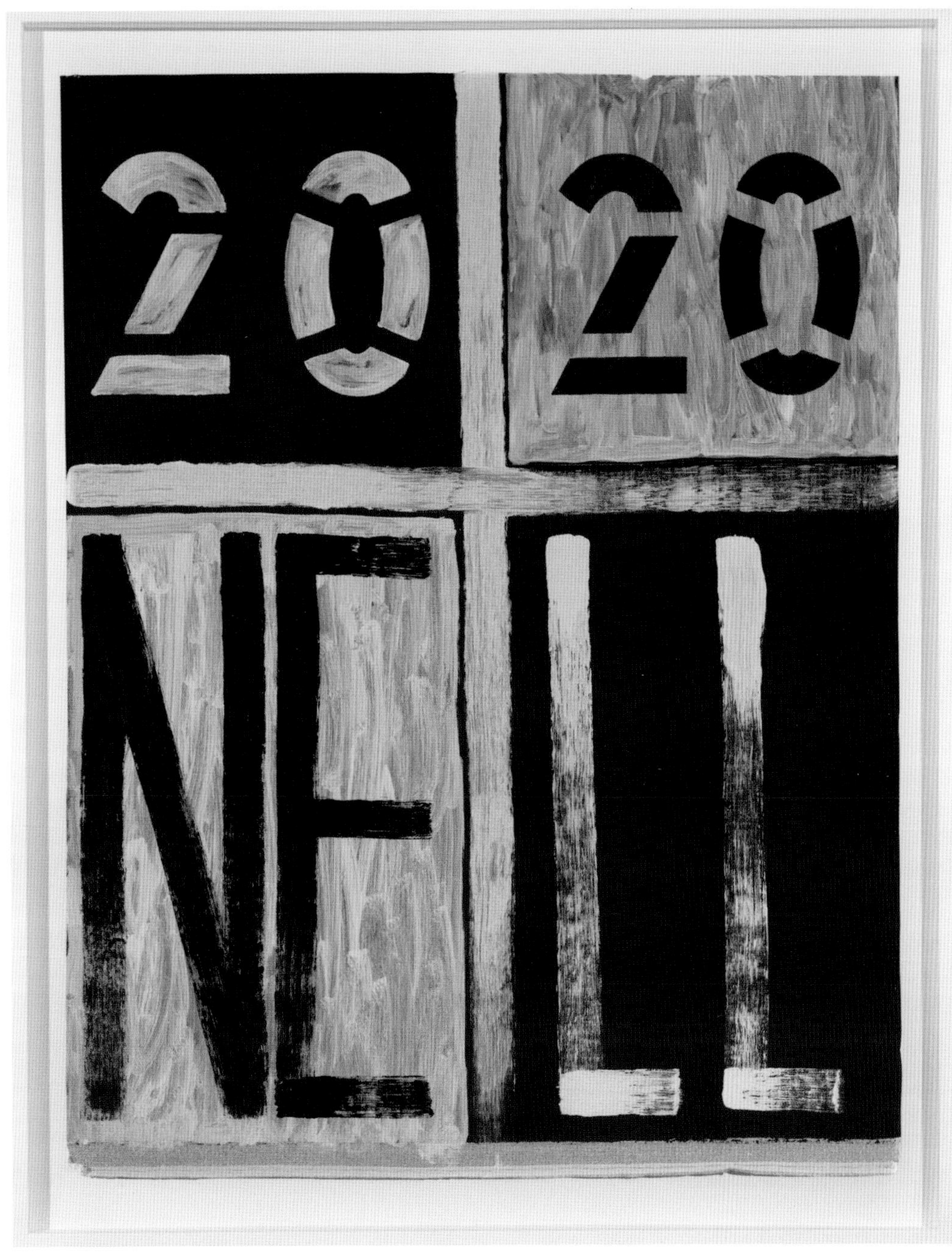

2020 NELL
2018

Don't You See?
2018

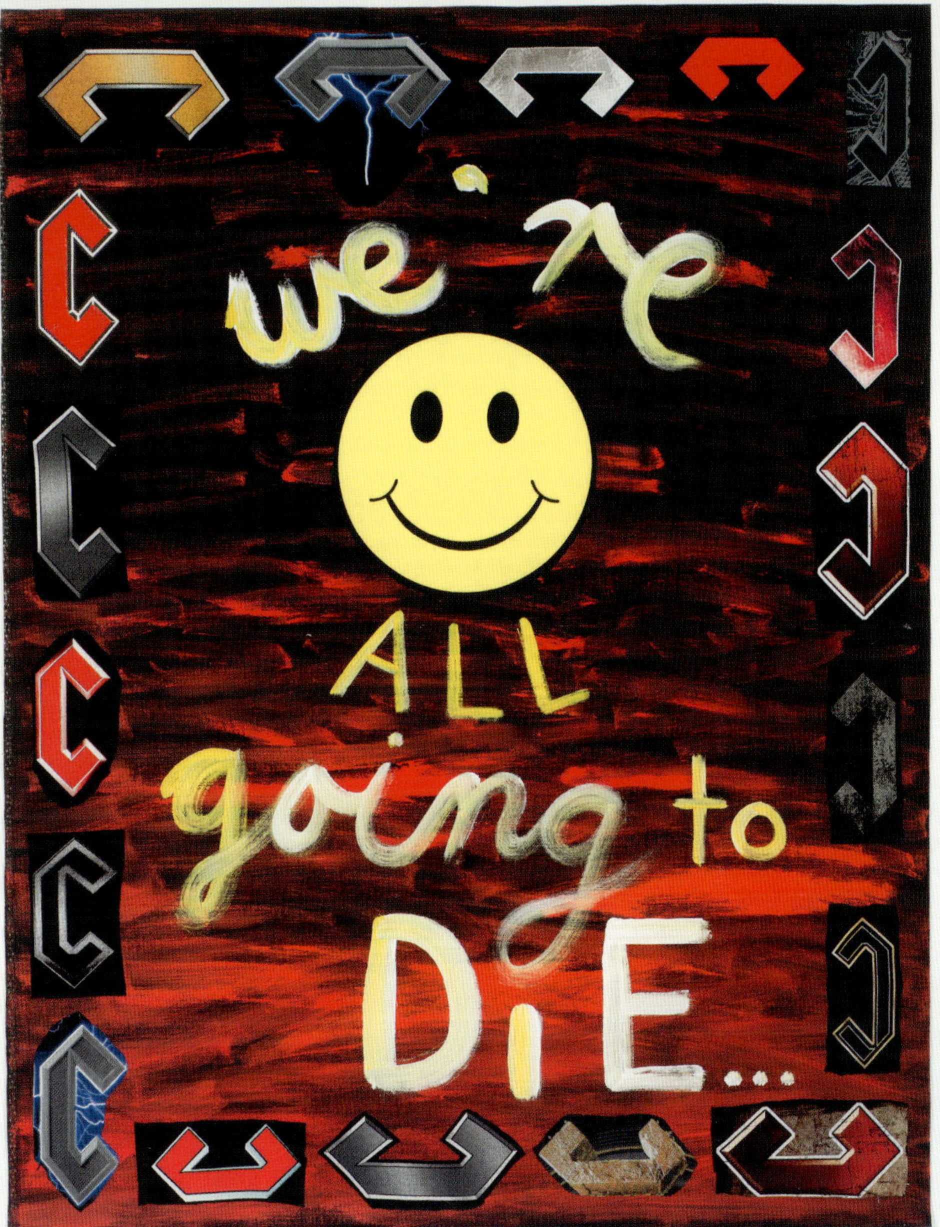
we're
ALL
going to
DiE...

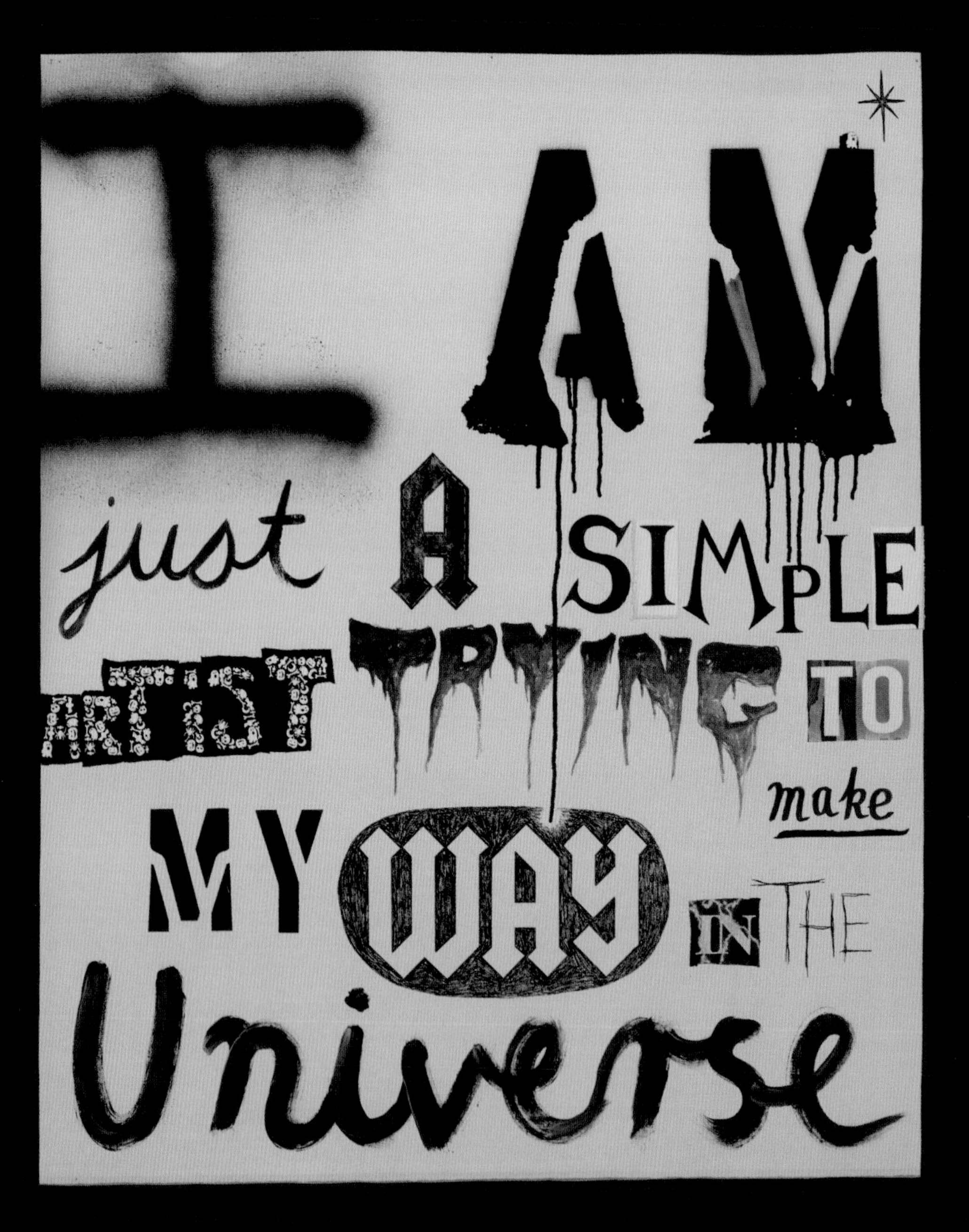

I AM just A SIMPLE ARTIST TRYING TO make MY WAY IN THE Universe
2018

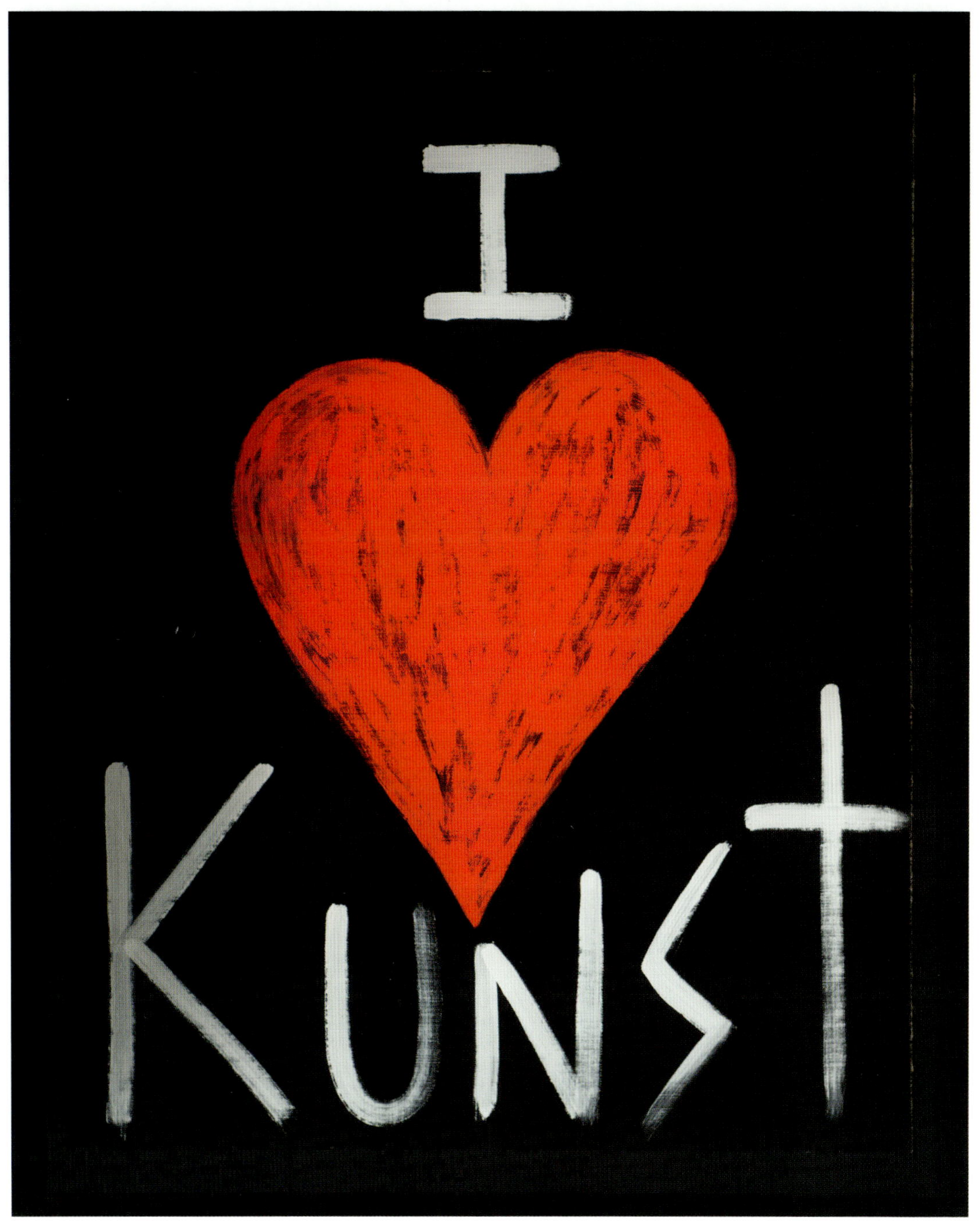

And KUNST Loves Me
2018

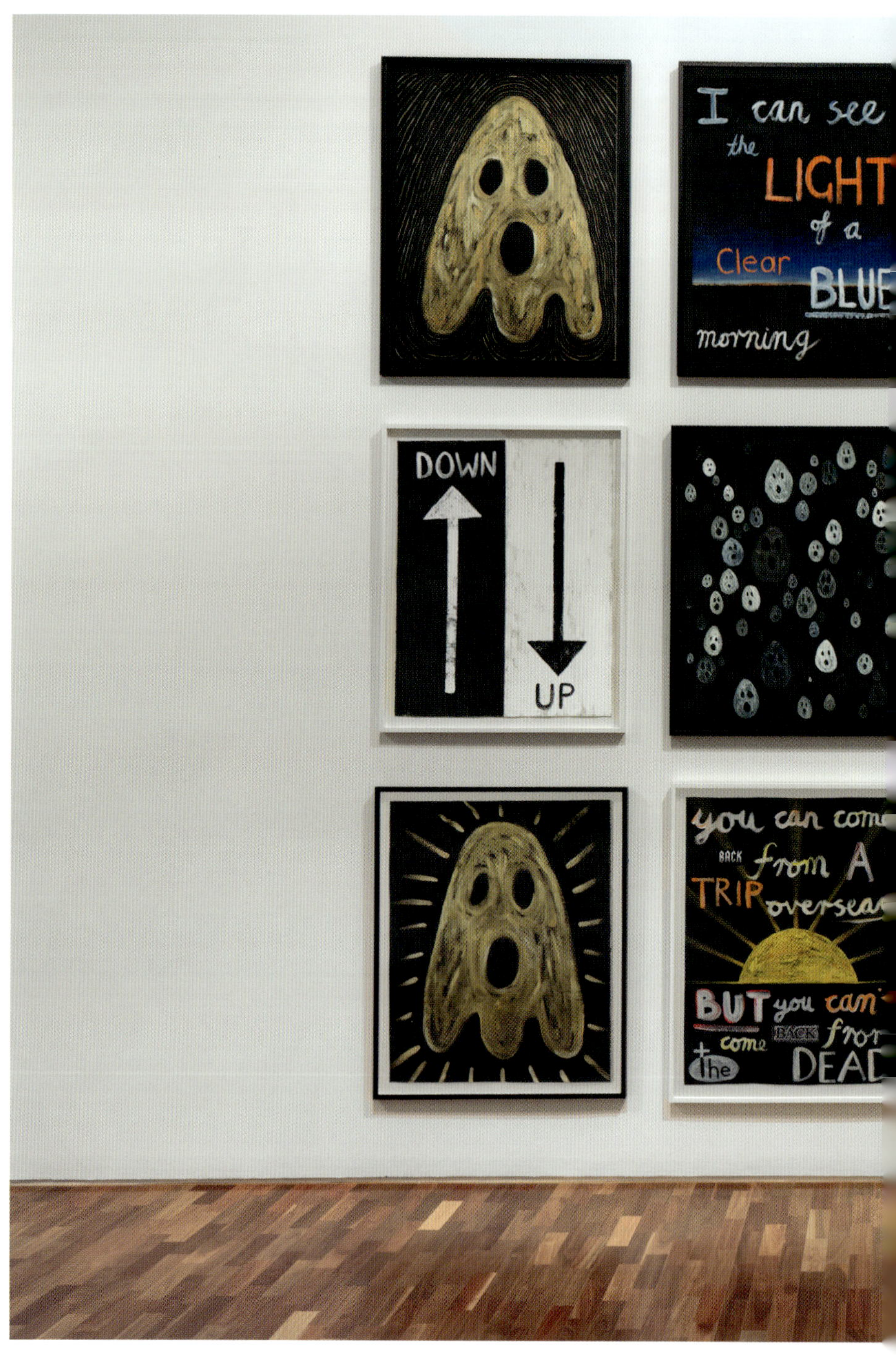

Blessings
2017–18

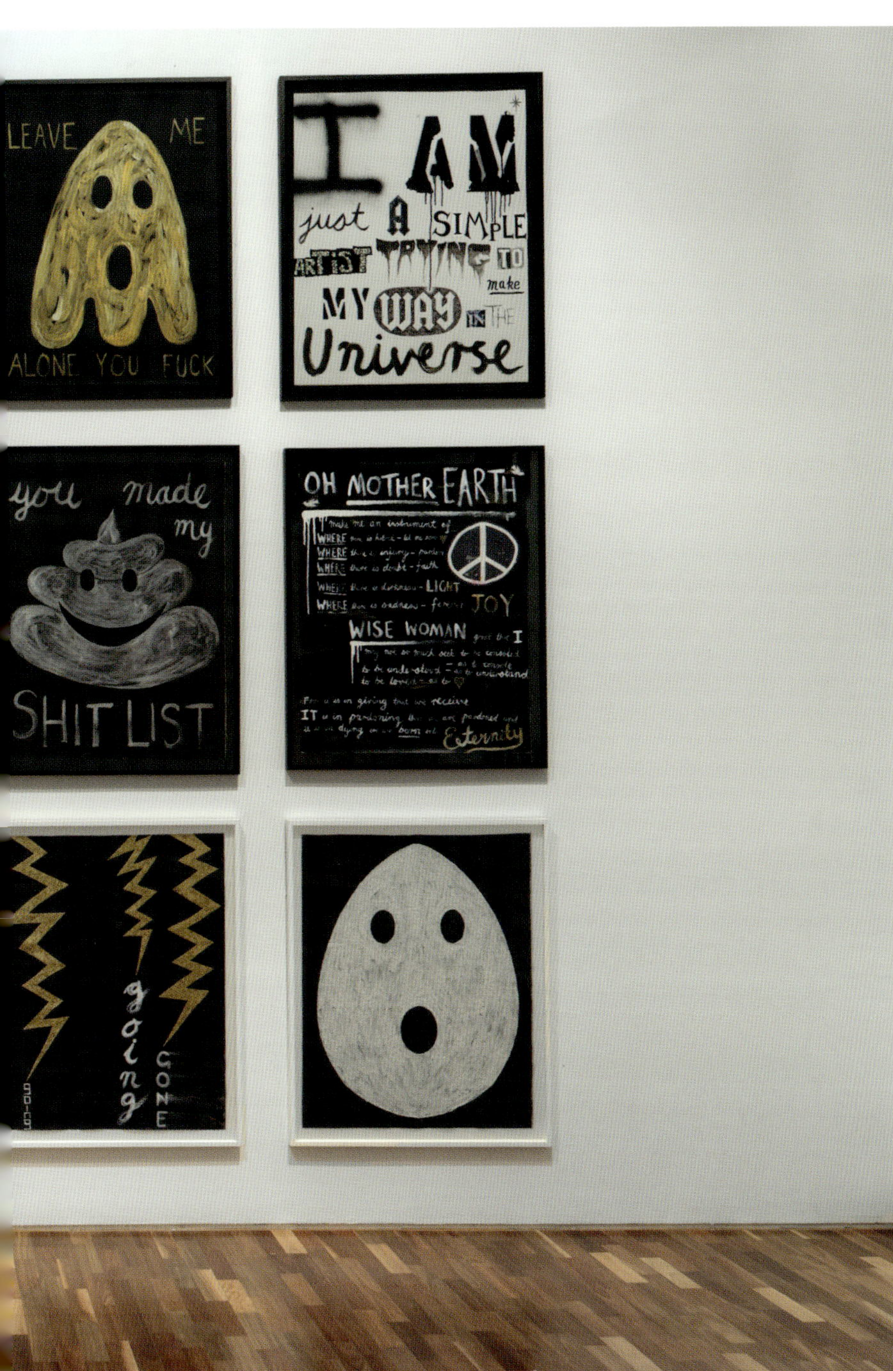
LEAVE ME
ALONE YOU FUCK
I AM just A SIMPLE ARTIST TRYING TO make MY WAY IN THE Universe
you made my
SHIT LIST
OH MOTHER EARTH
LIGHT
JOY
WISE WOMAN
Eternity
going
going
GONE

a white bird flies in the mist, a black bird flies in the night,
a woman walks, wild and free, she is not afraid to die
2008

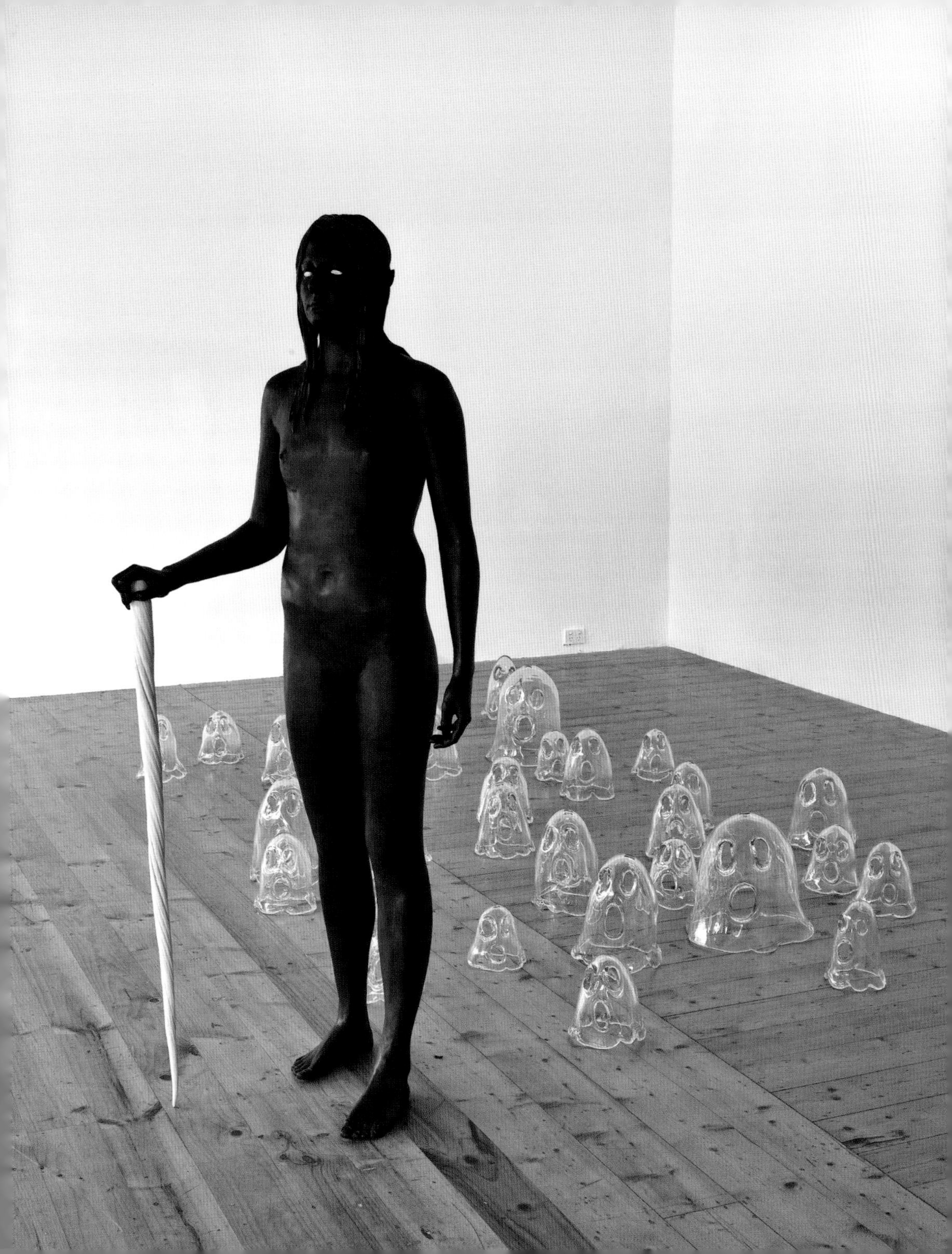

Mother and Child #2
2017

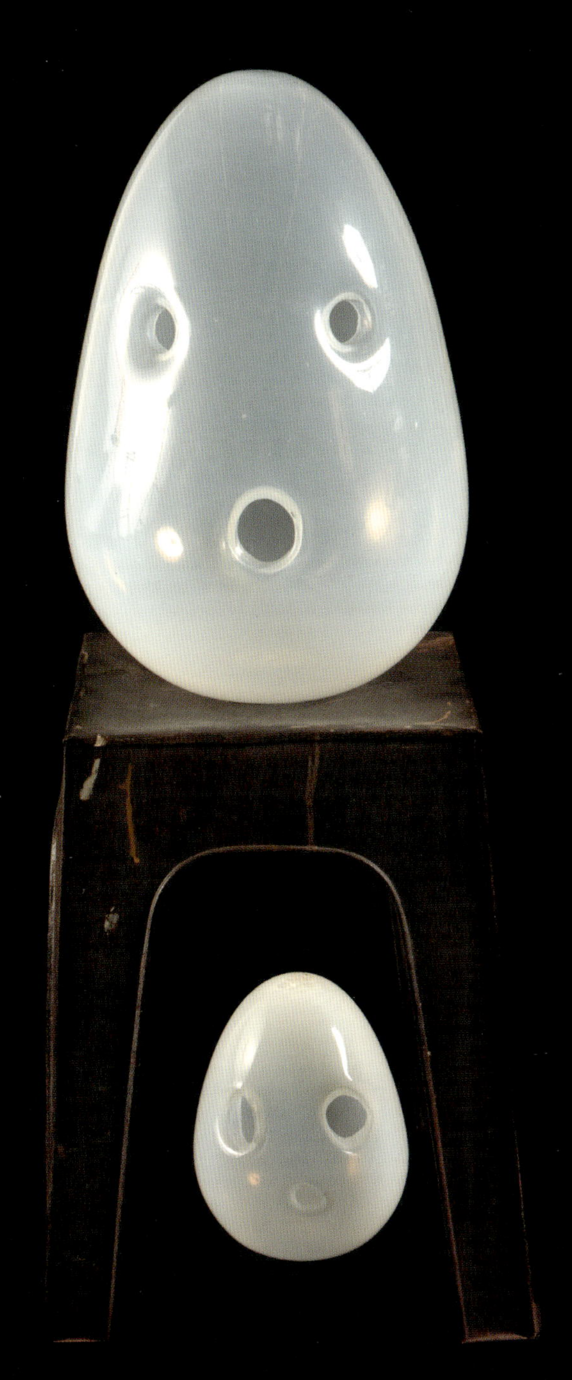

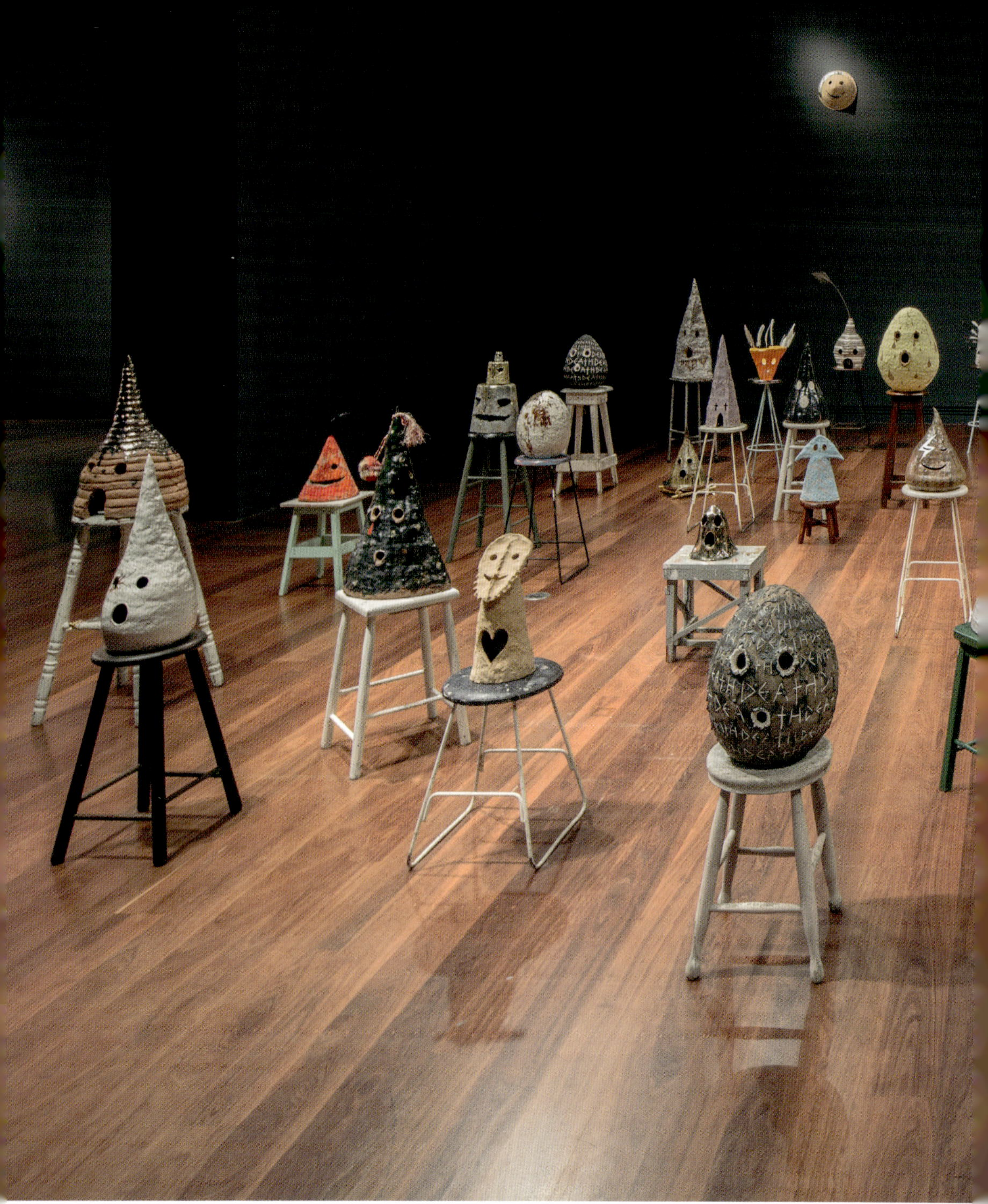

The Wake
2014–16

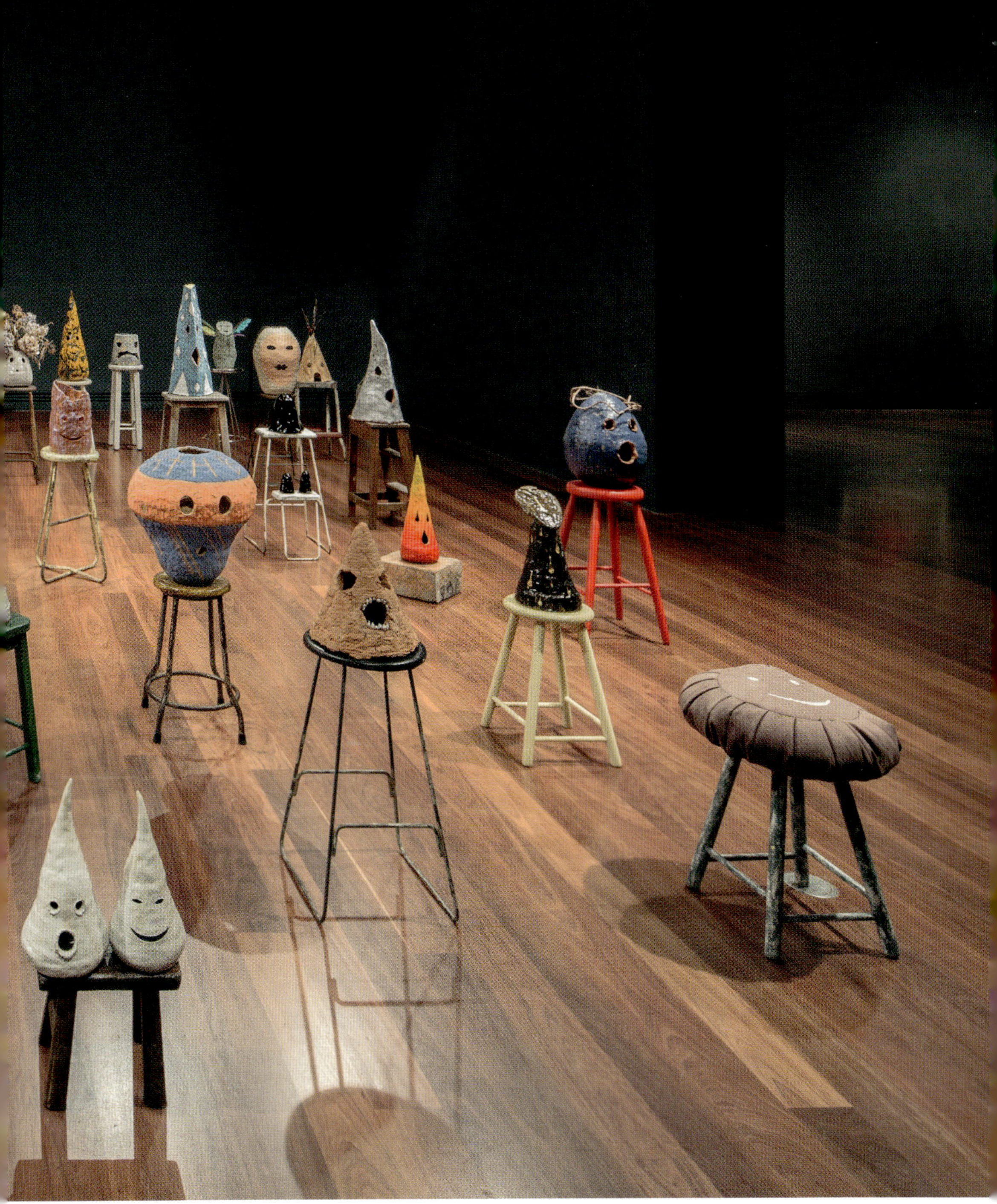

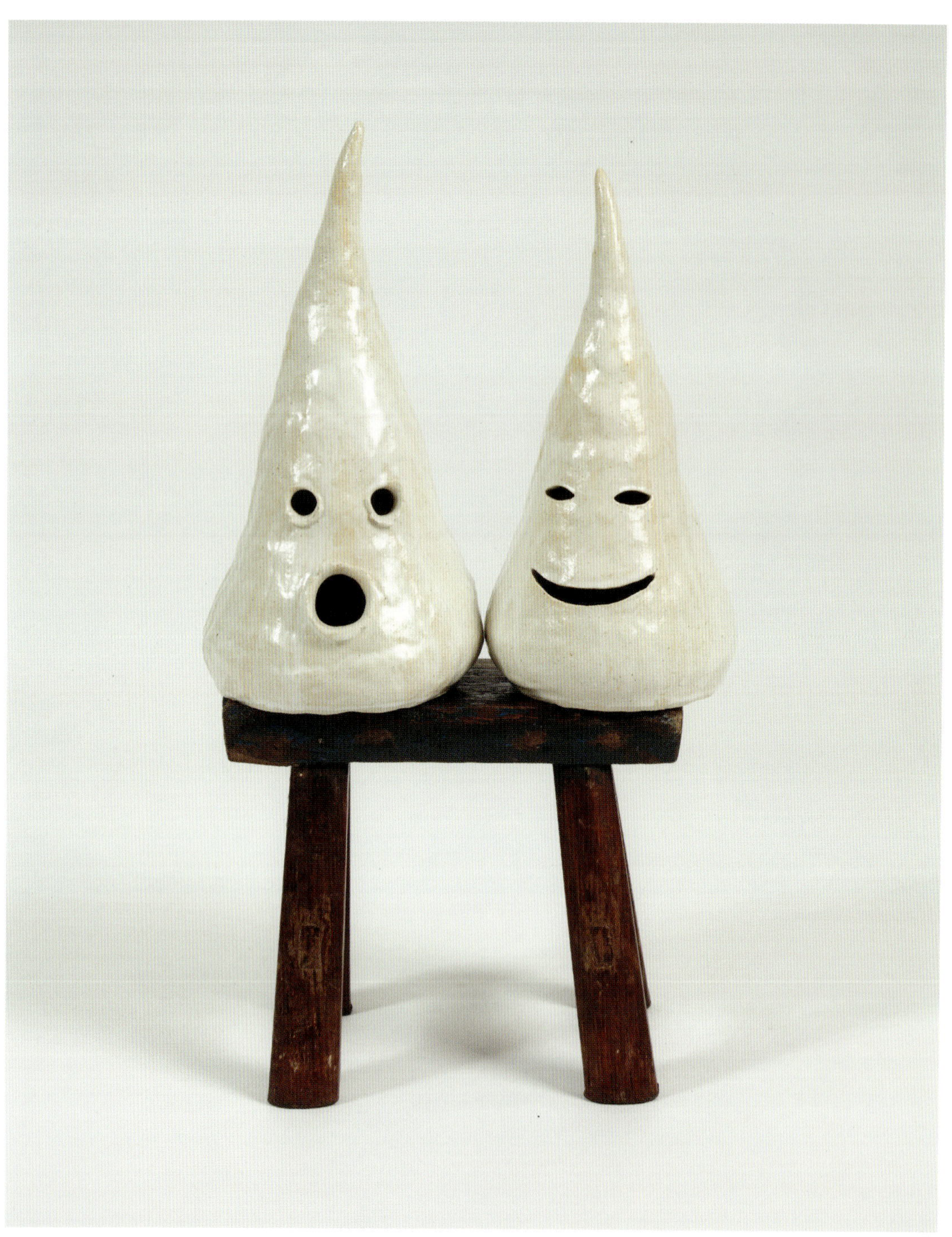

History is Now
2014–15

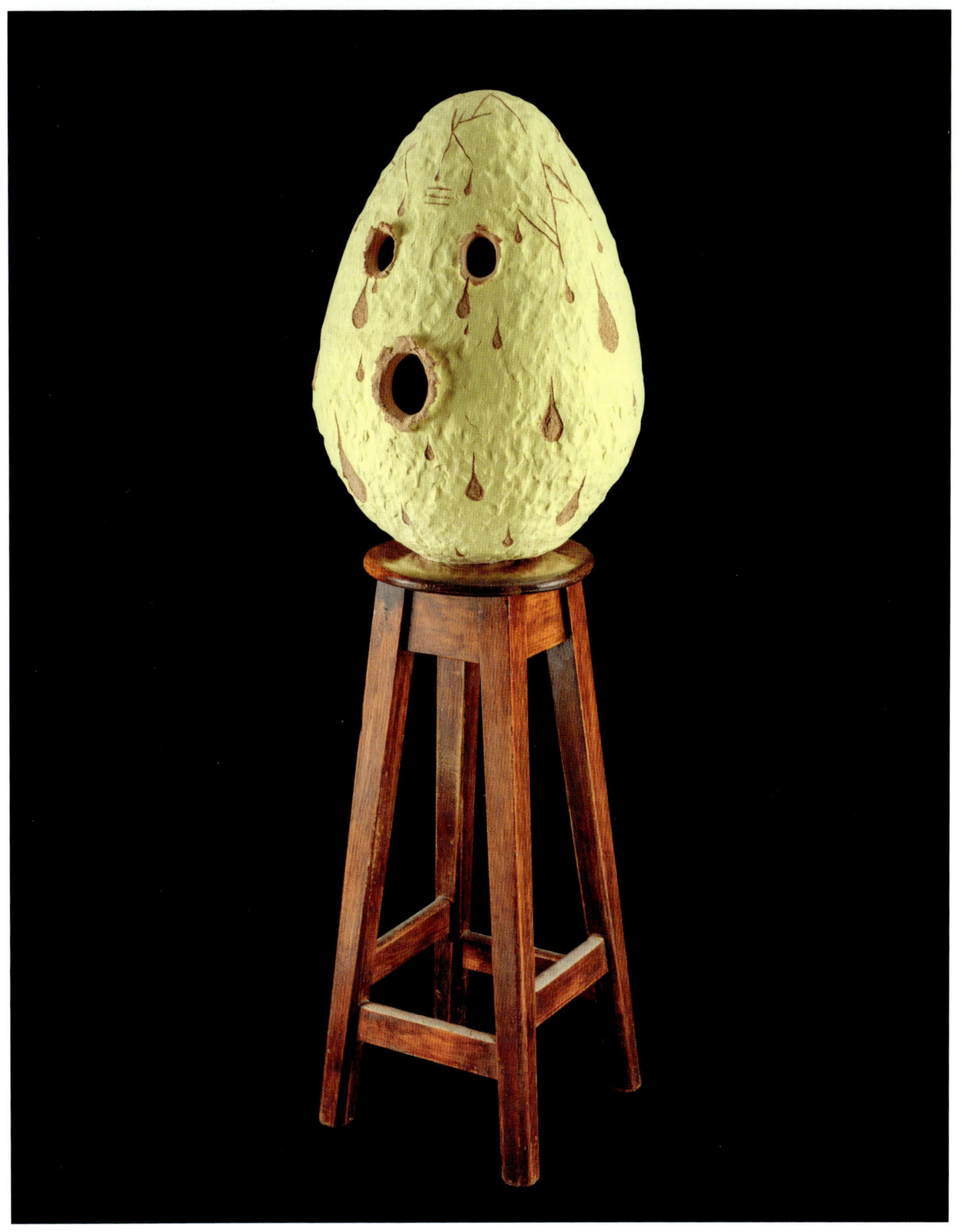

3 words and good BYE
2015–16

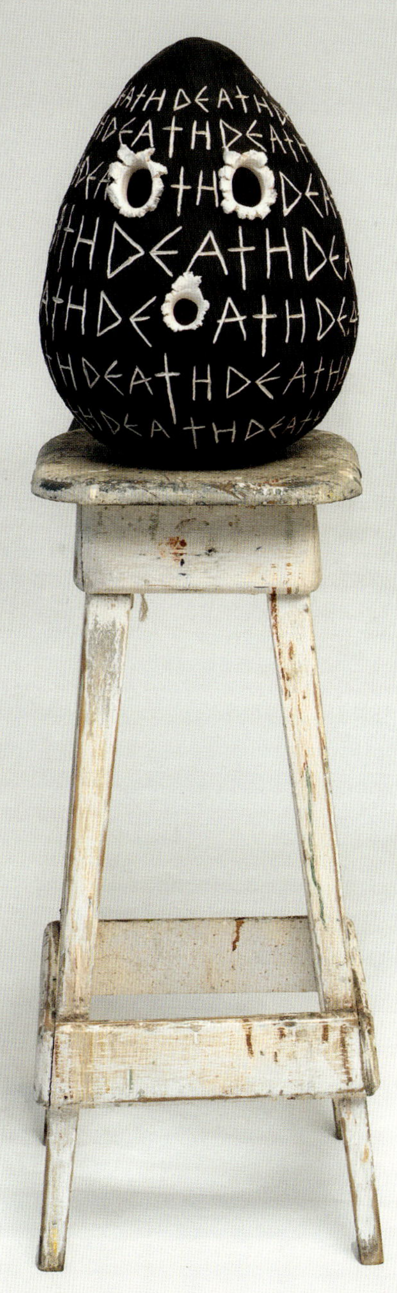

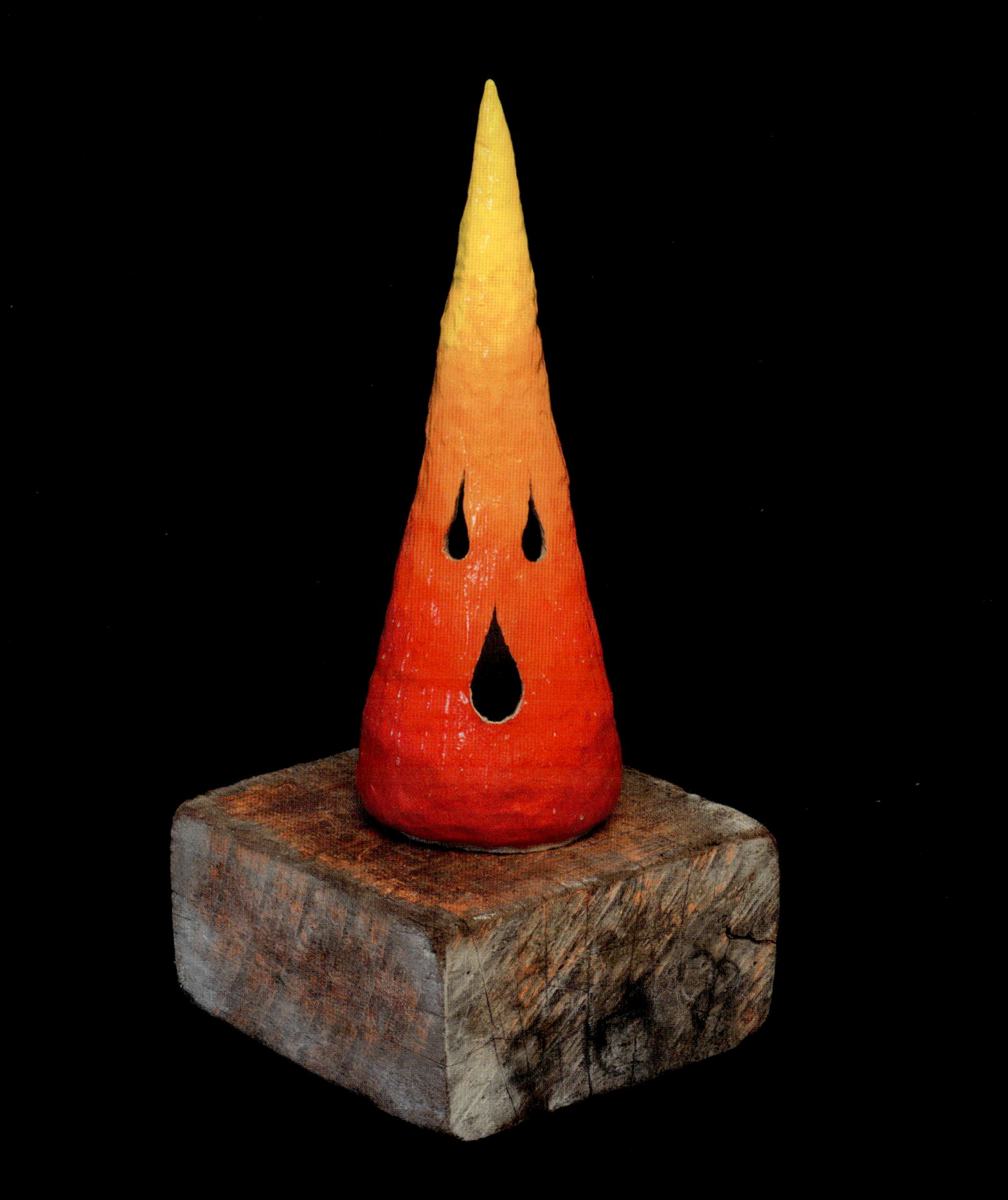

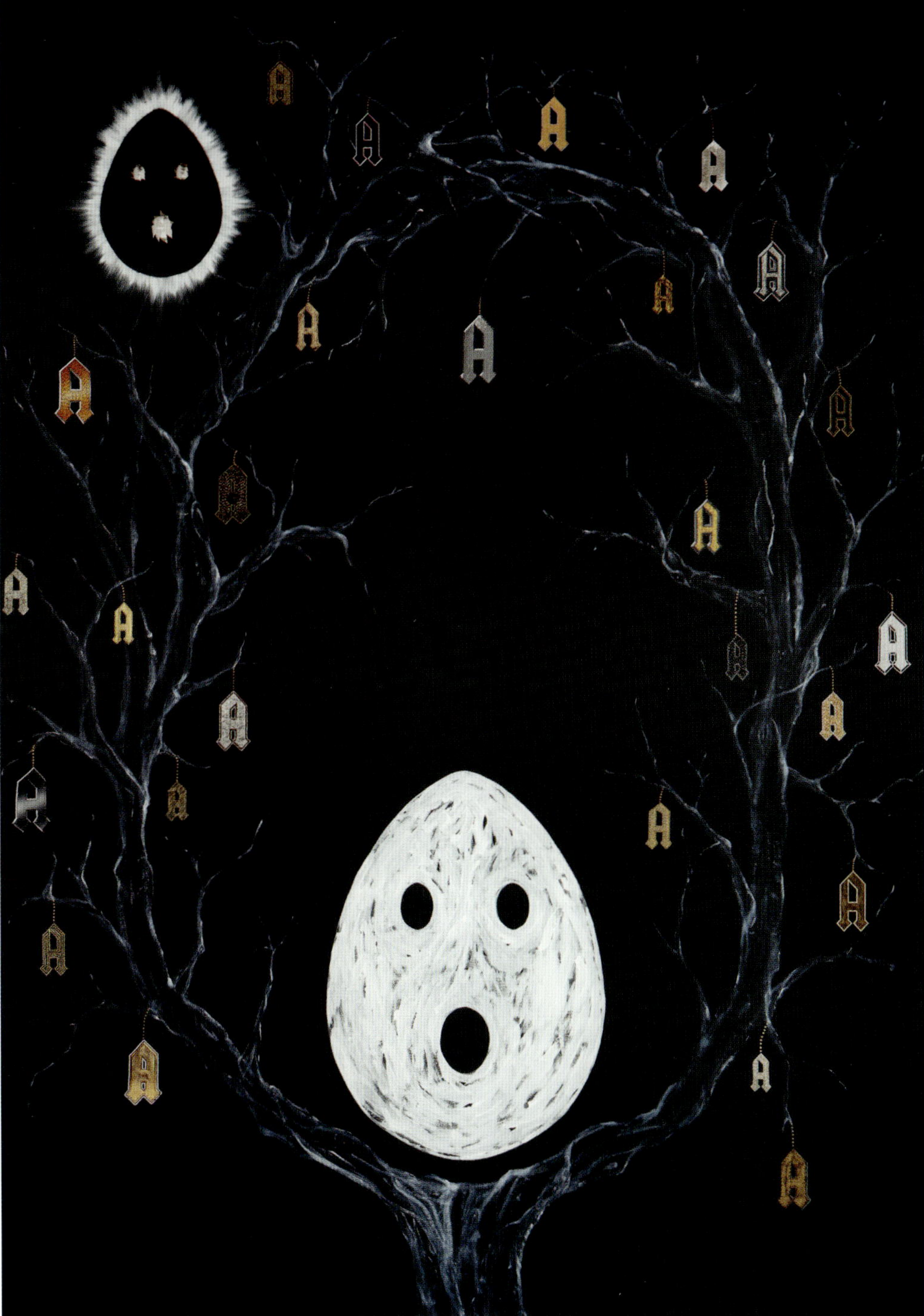

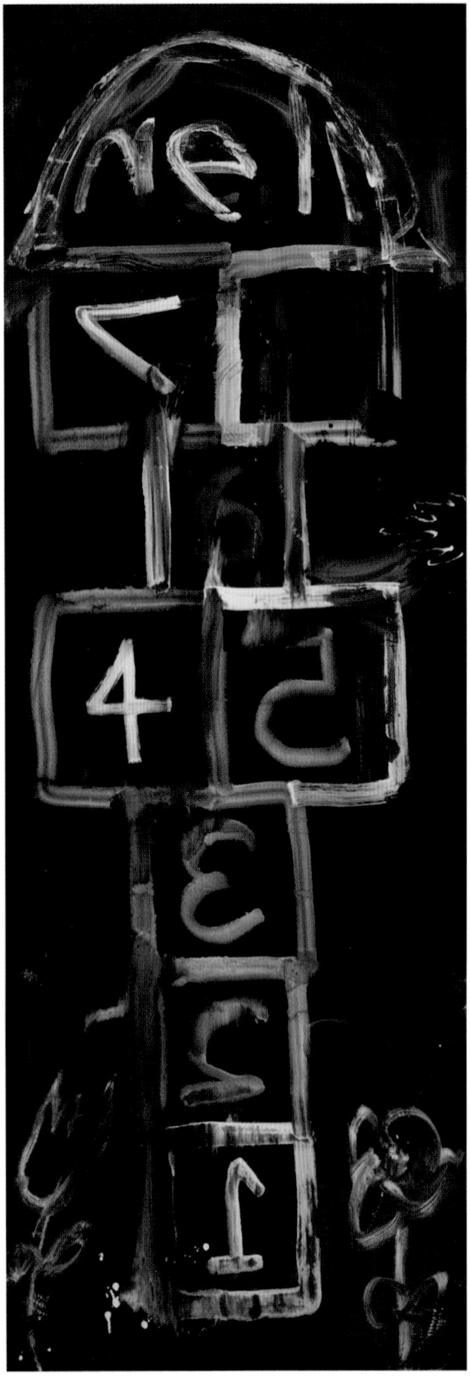

1, 2, 3, 4, 5, 6, 7, 8, nell (washed away)
2010

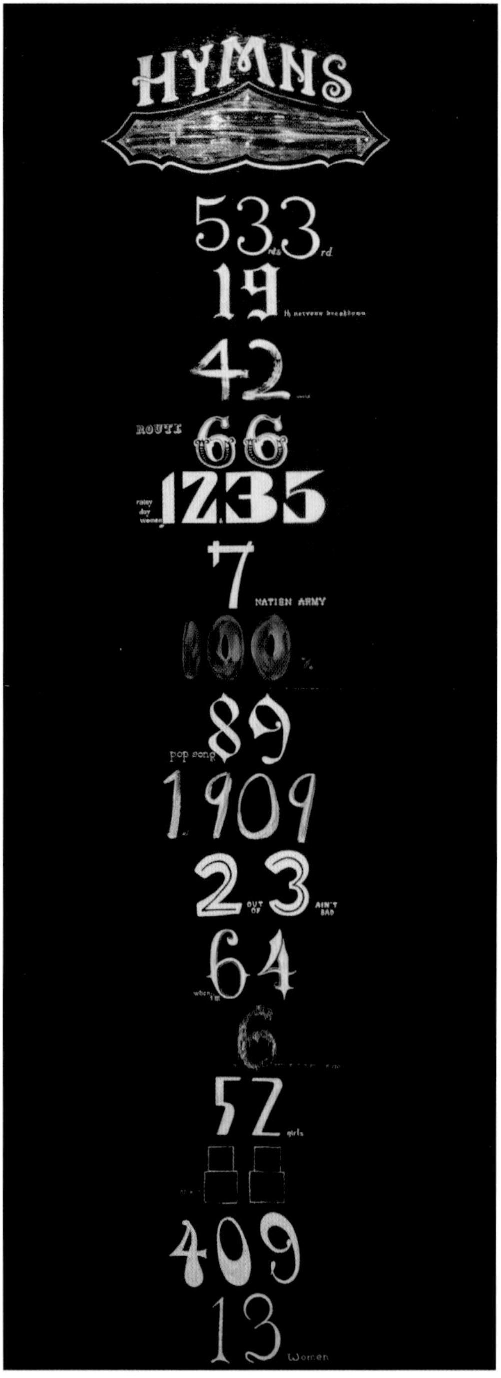

singing from the same hymn book – the songs the Lord taught us
2010

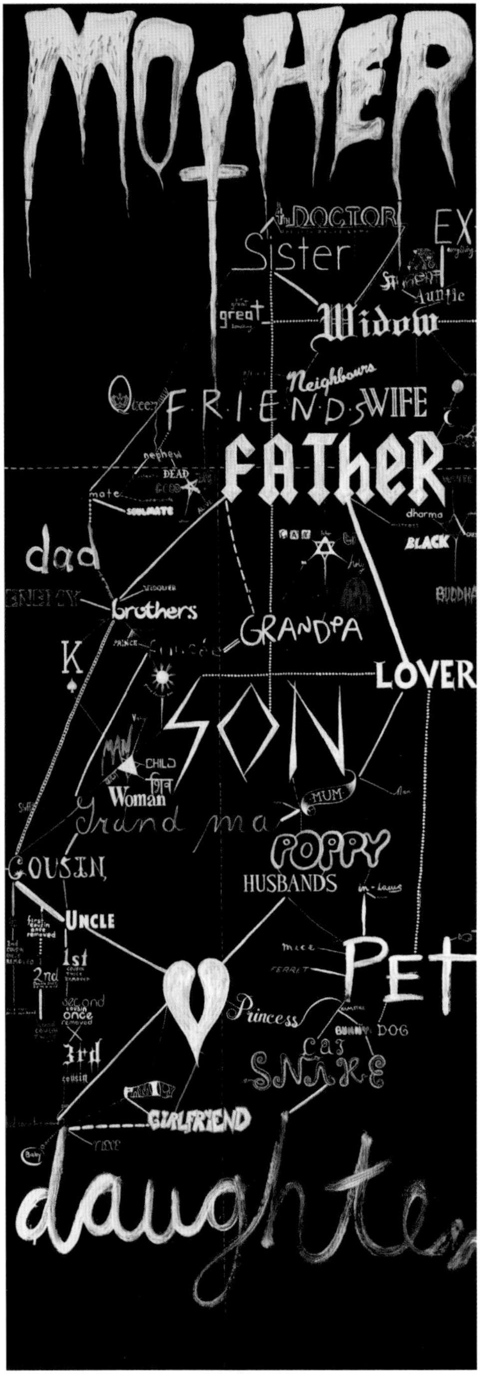

from mother to daughter – all relationships are endless
2010

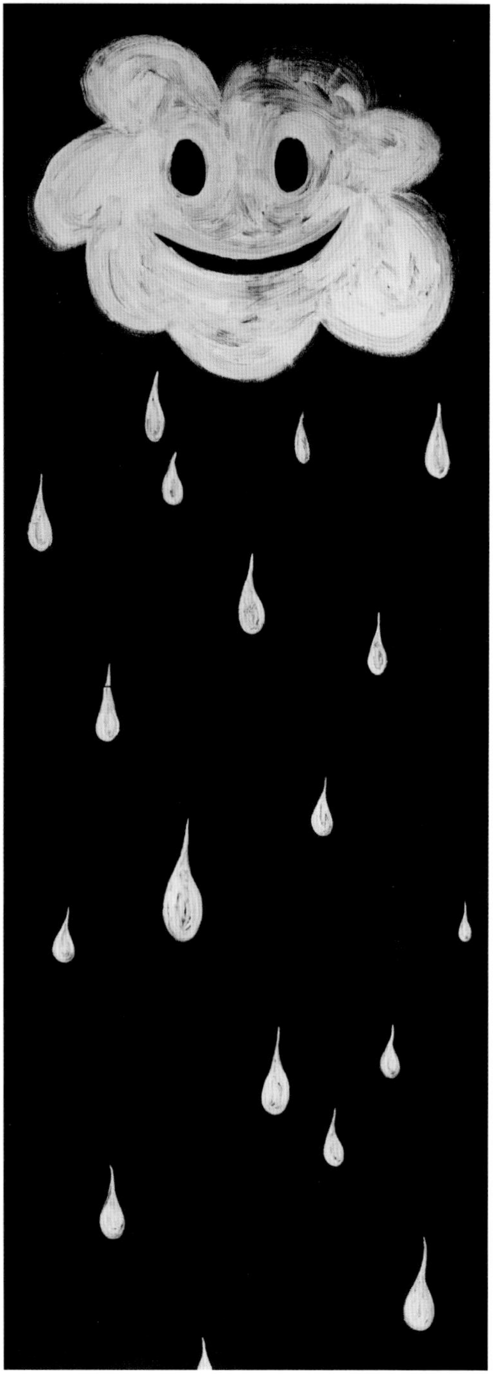

one happy cloud – many raindrips
2010

Made in the Light – Happy Cloud and Drips
2011

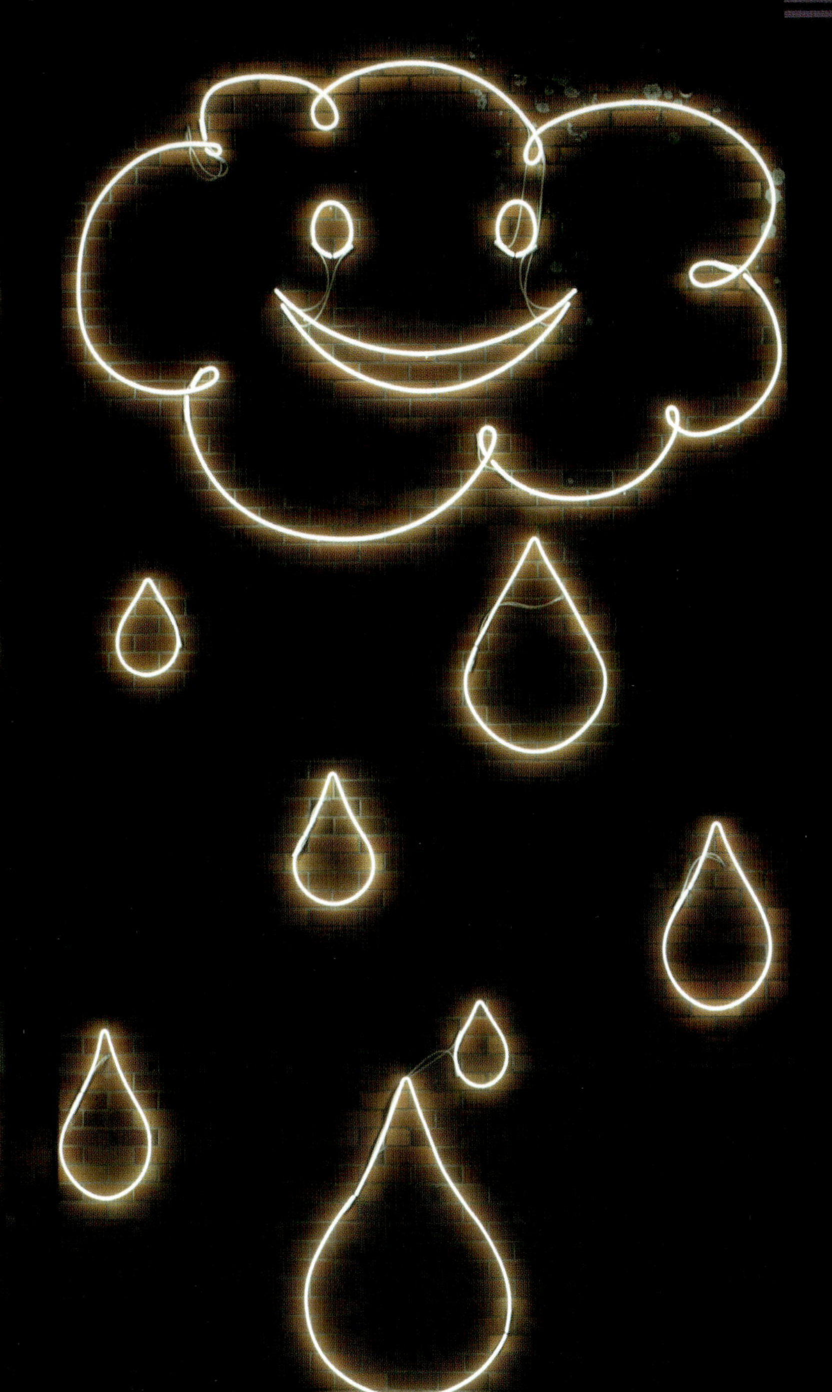

The Ghost Who Walks will Never Die
2005

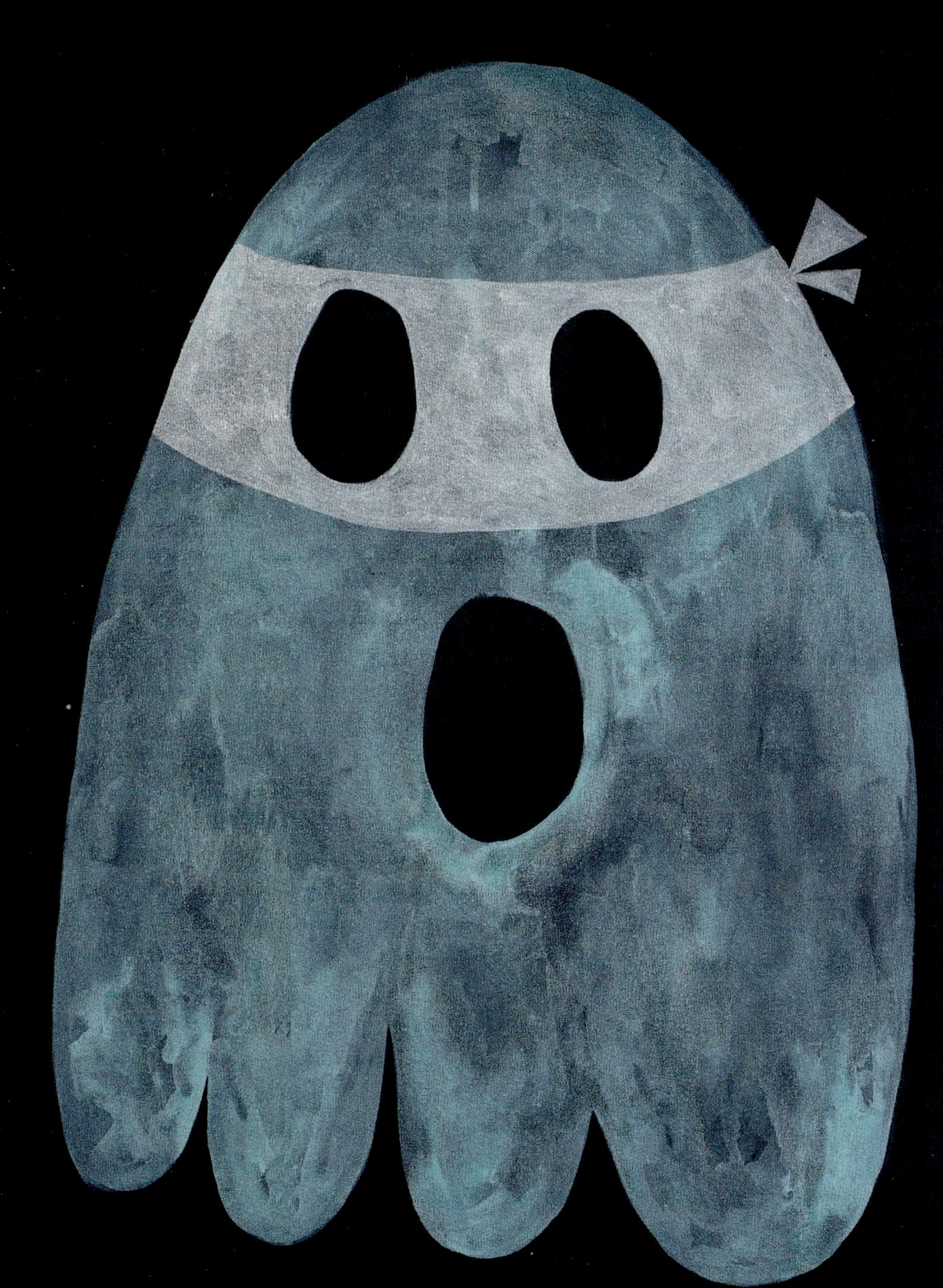

Who Made Who
2004

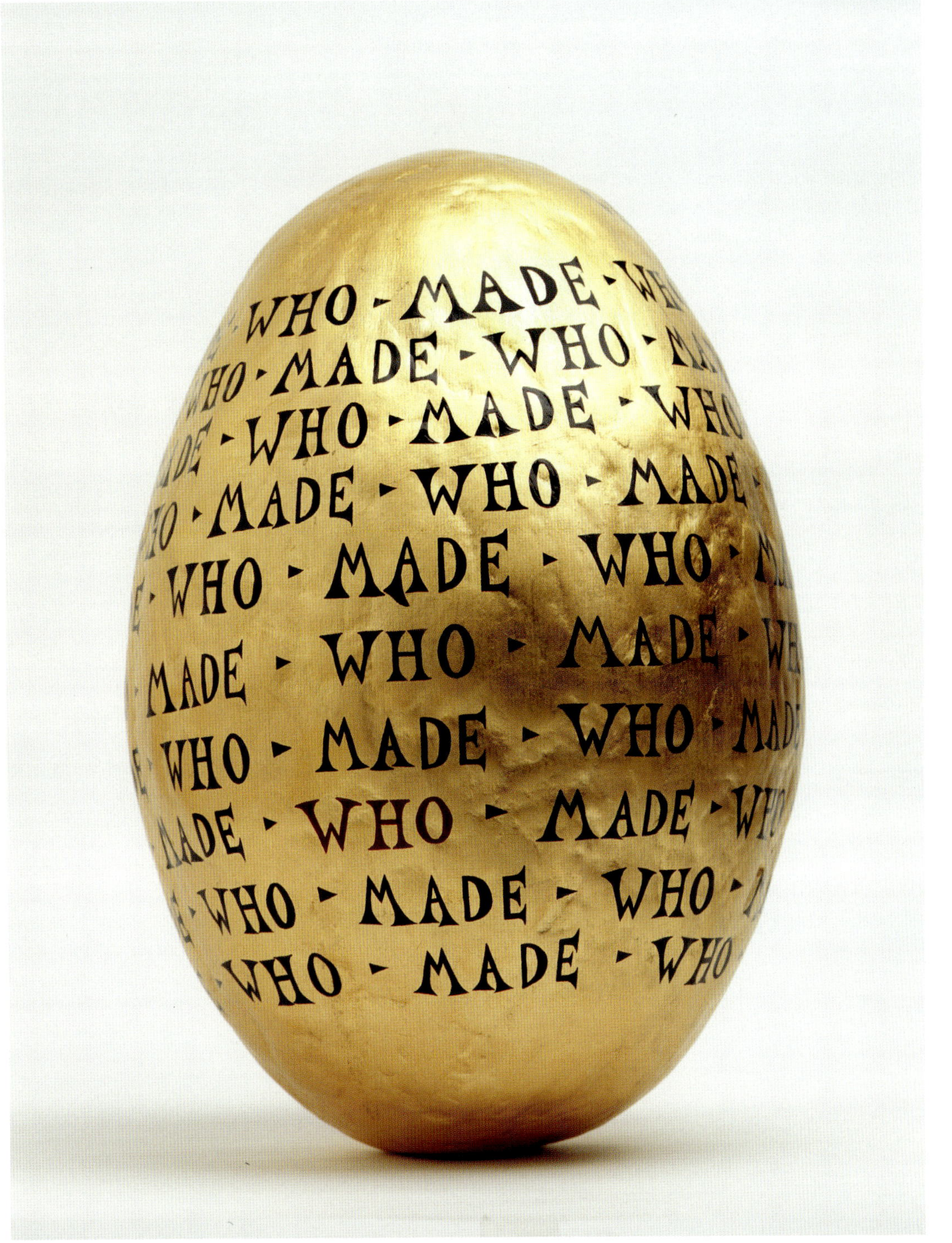

WHO · MADE ·
MADE · WHO ·
WHO · MADE ·
MADE · WHO · MADE
WHO · MADE · WHO ·
MADE · WHO · MADE ·
WHO · MADE · WHO ·
MADE · WHO · MADE ·
WHO · MADE · WHO ·
WHO · MADE · WHO

The Dr. said it was like being hit by lightning
2013

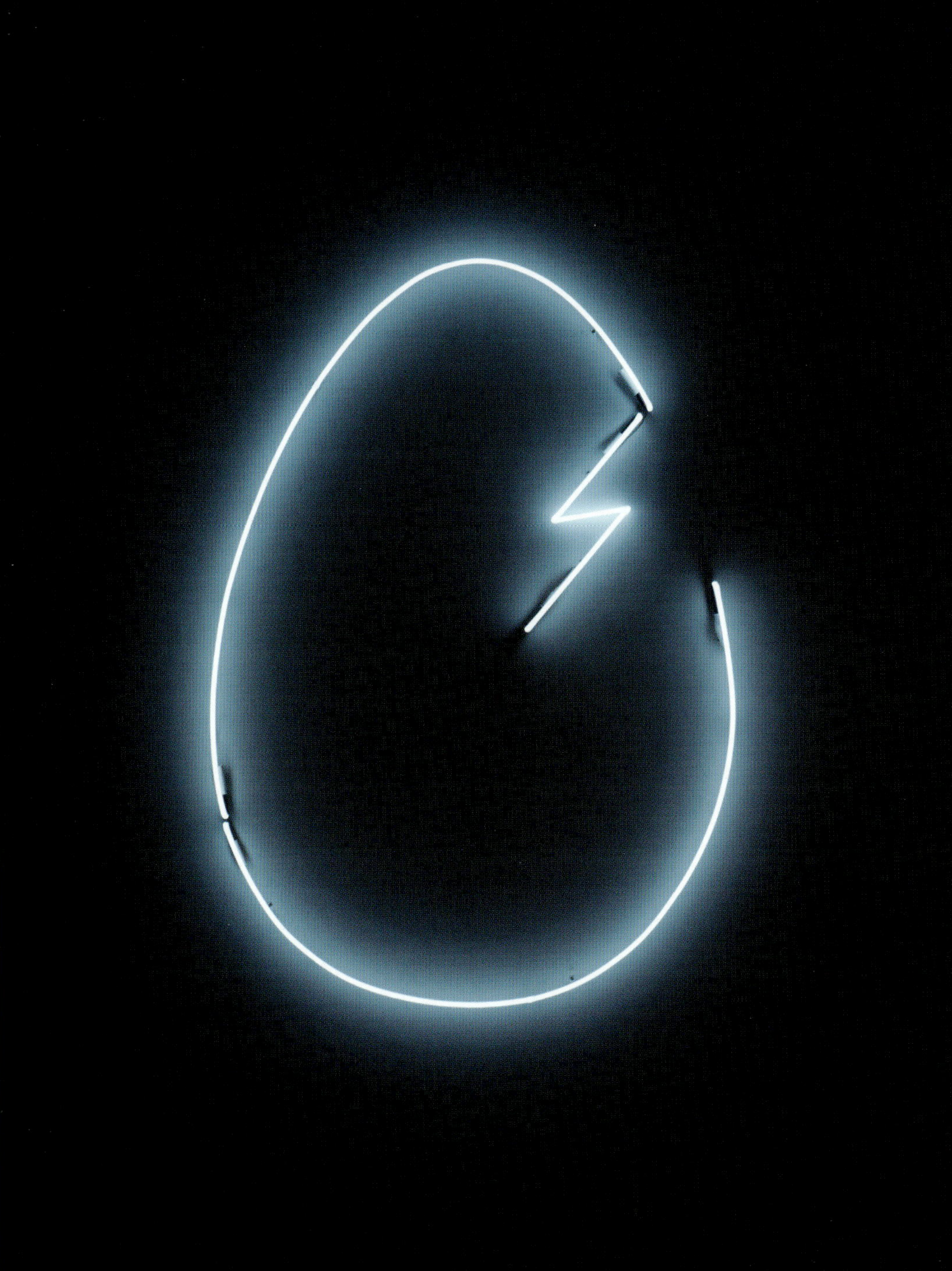

Let R.I.P
2013

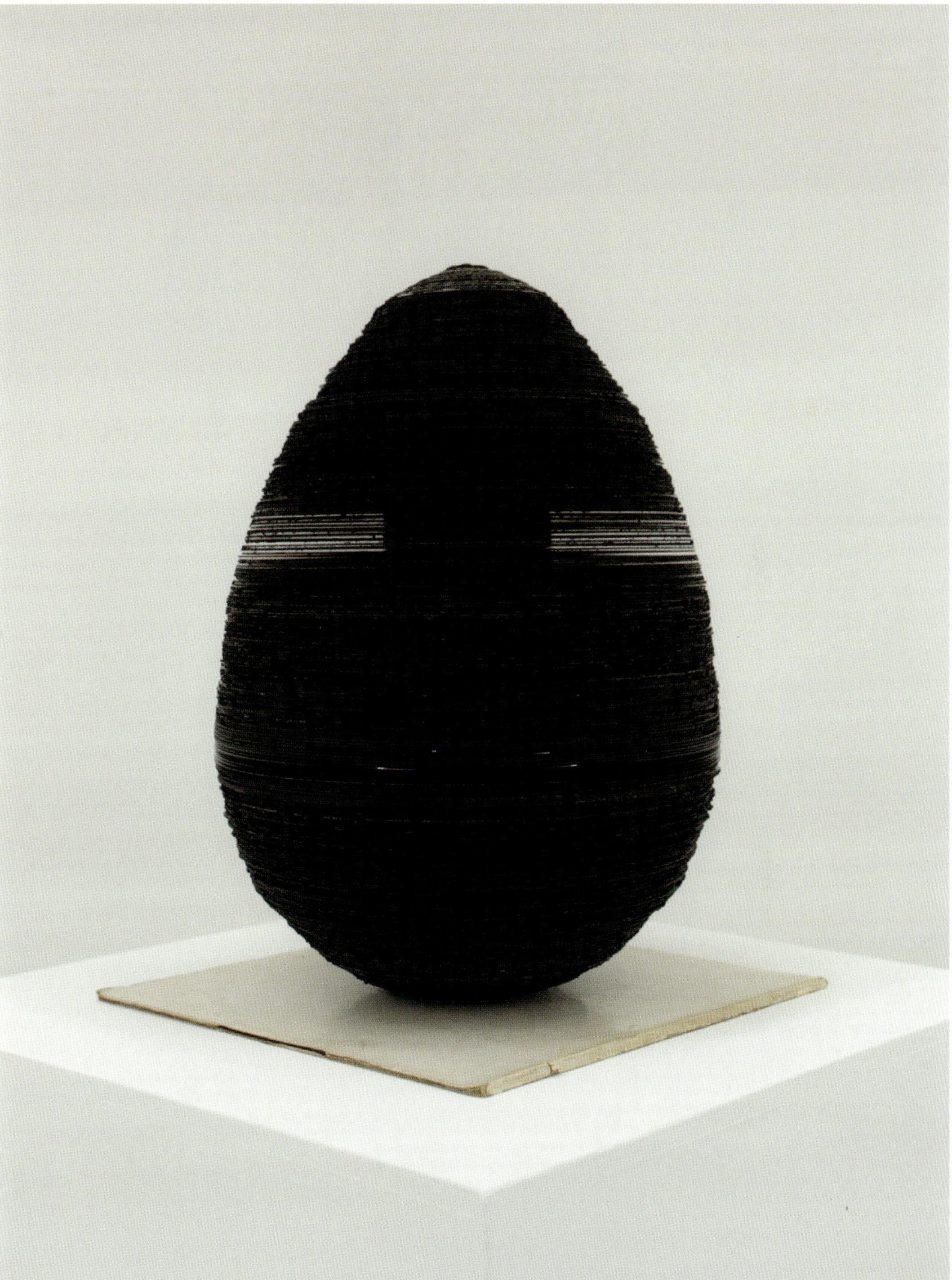

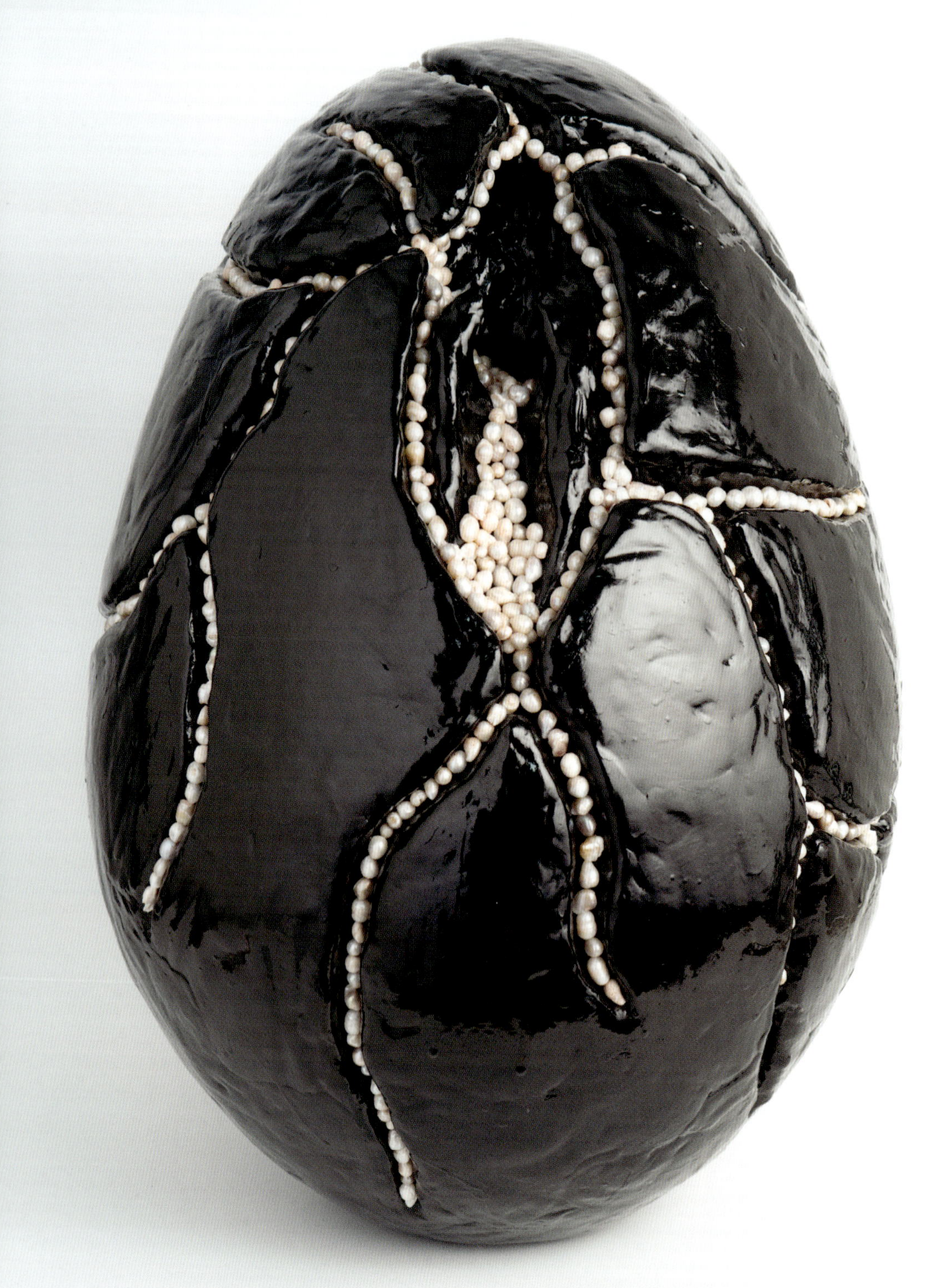

the gateless, pearly gate
2010

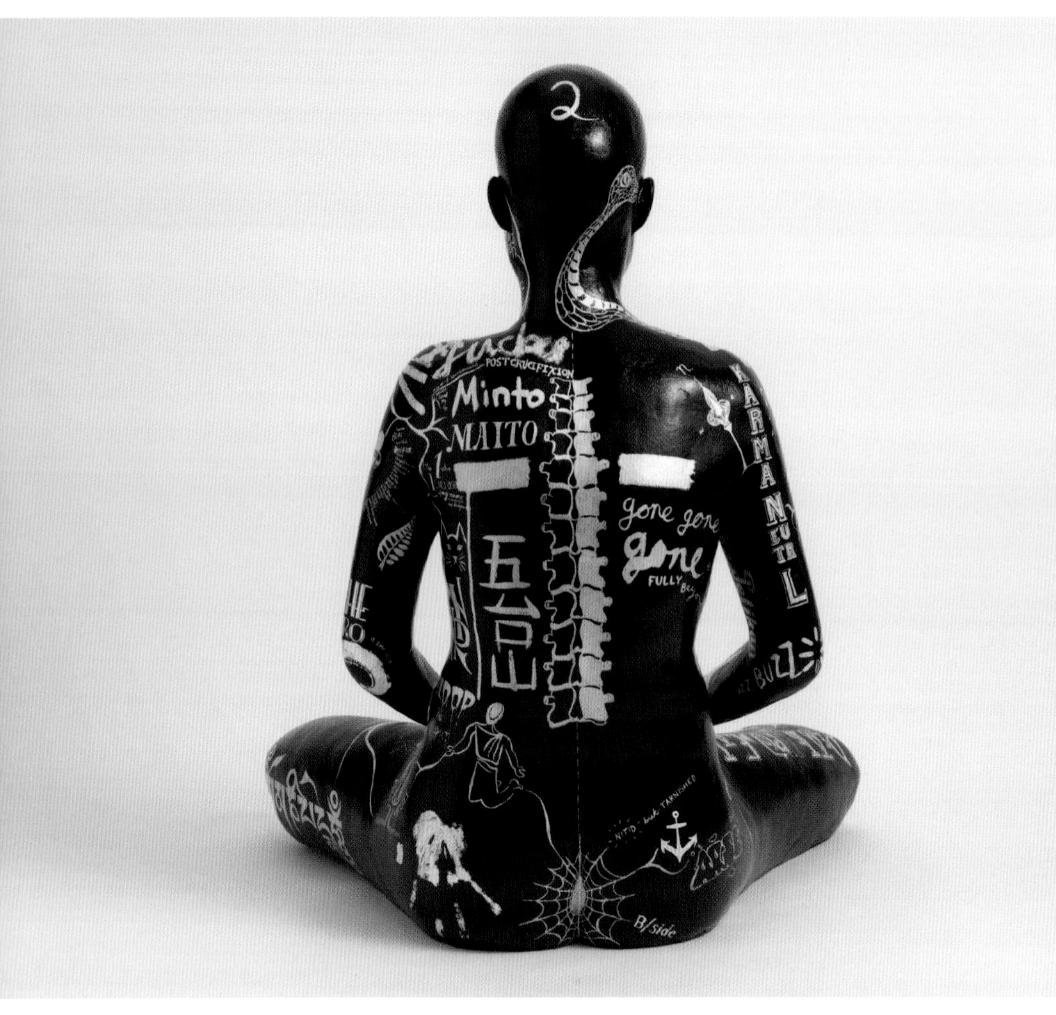

self-nature is subtle and mysterious – nun.sex.monk.rock
2010

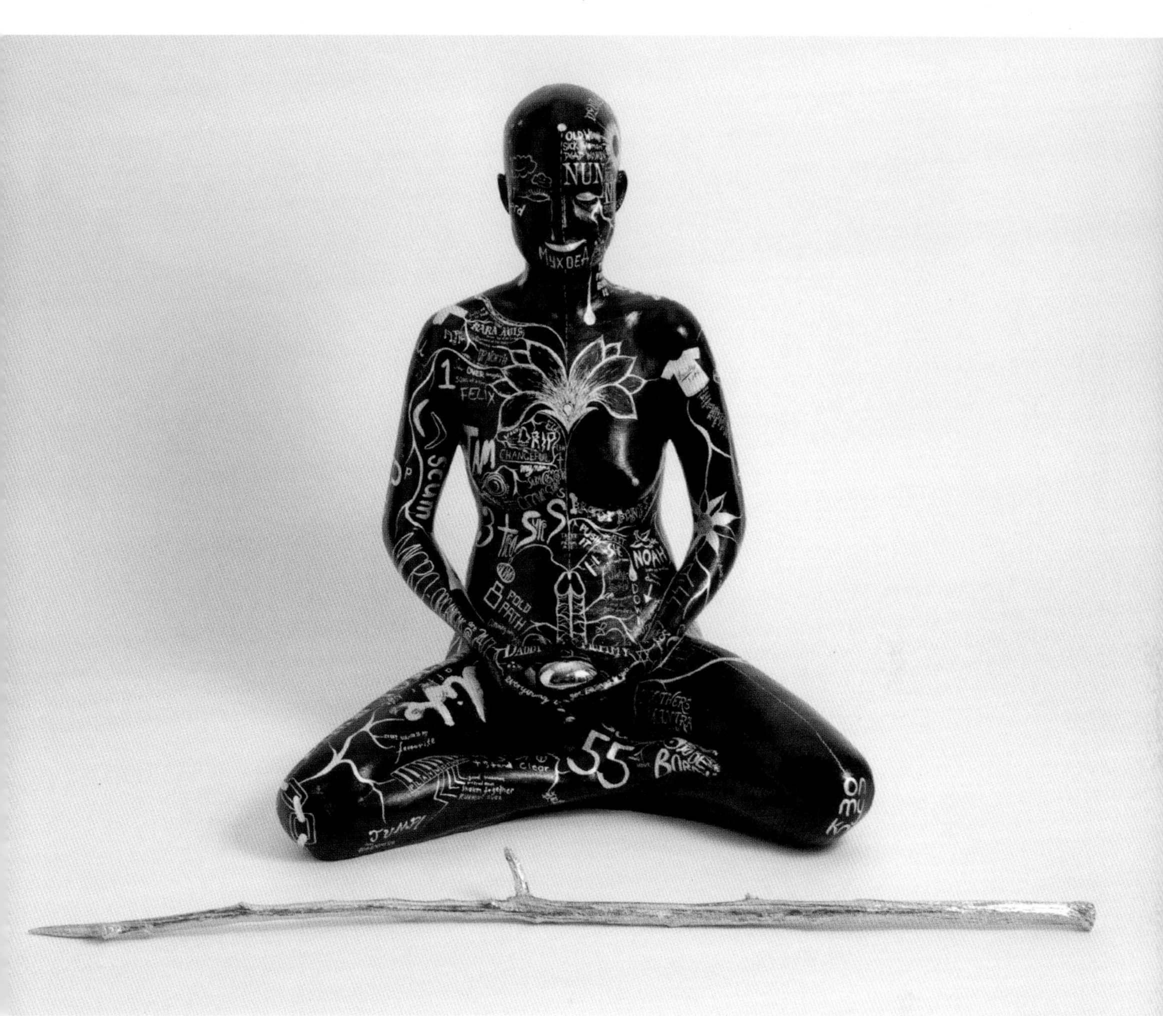
NUN
FELIX
DRIP
CHANGEFUL
NOAH
55
JUMP

More Sound Hours Than Can Ever Be Repaid – Back in Black, #4, 1980/2013
2013

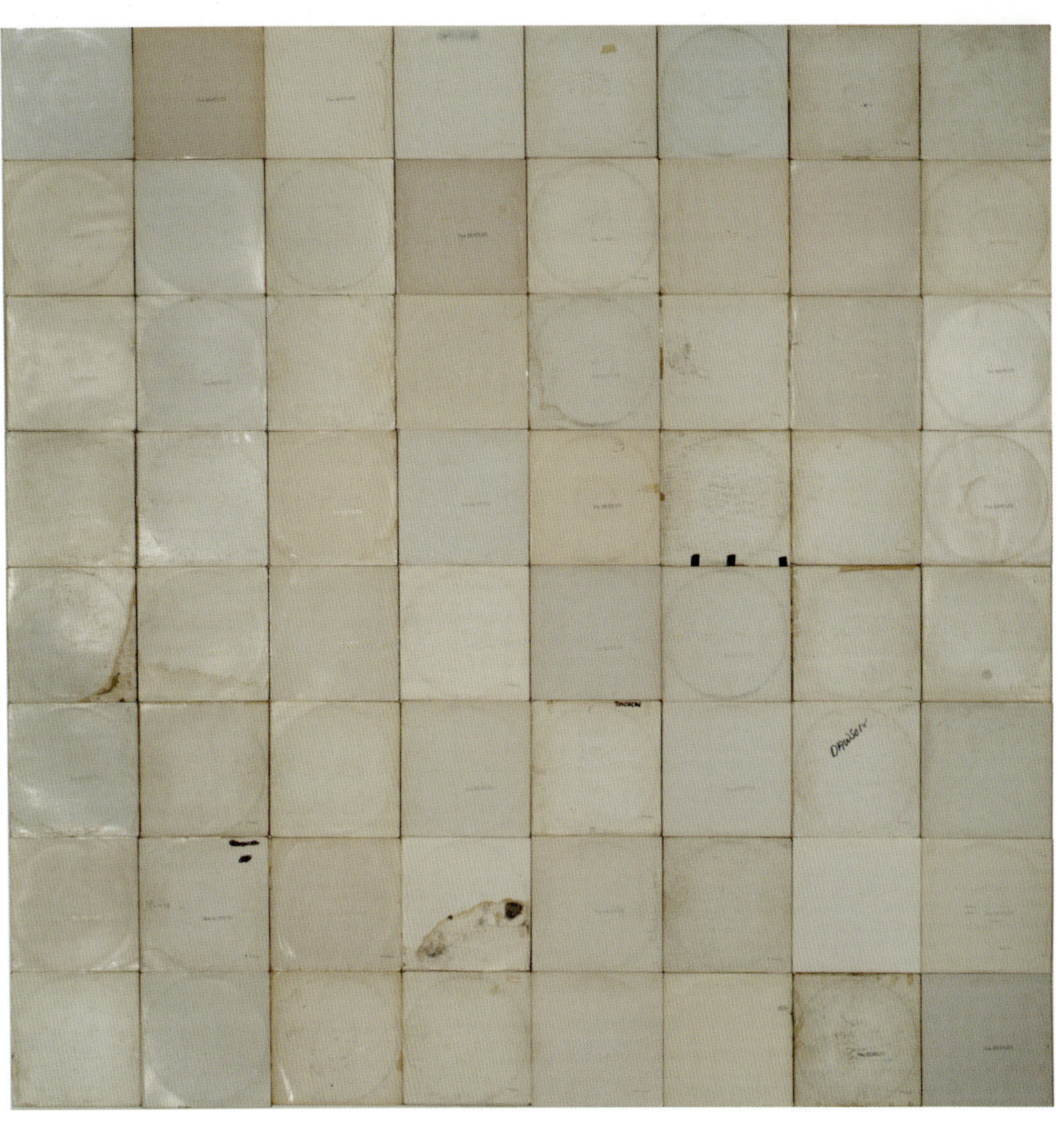

More Sound Hours Than Can Ever Be Repaid – The White Album, #1, 1968/2013
2013

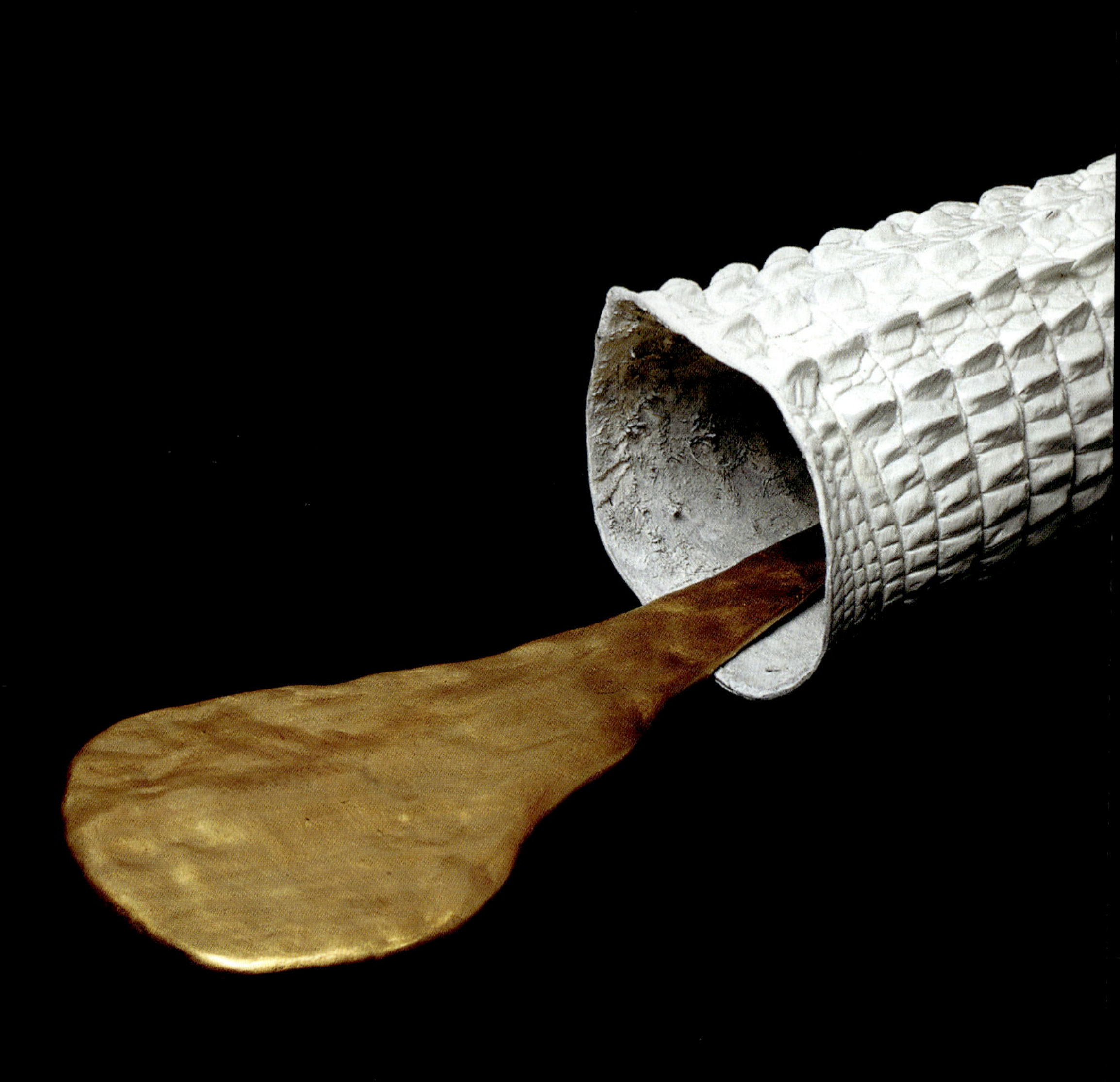

Not Without My Tail
2004

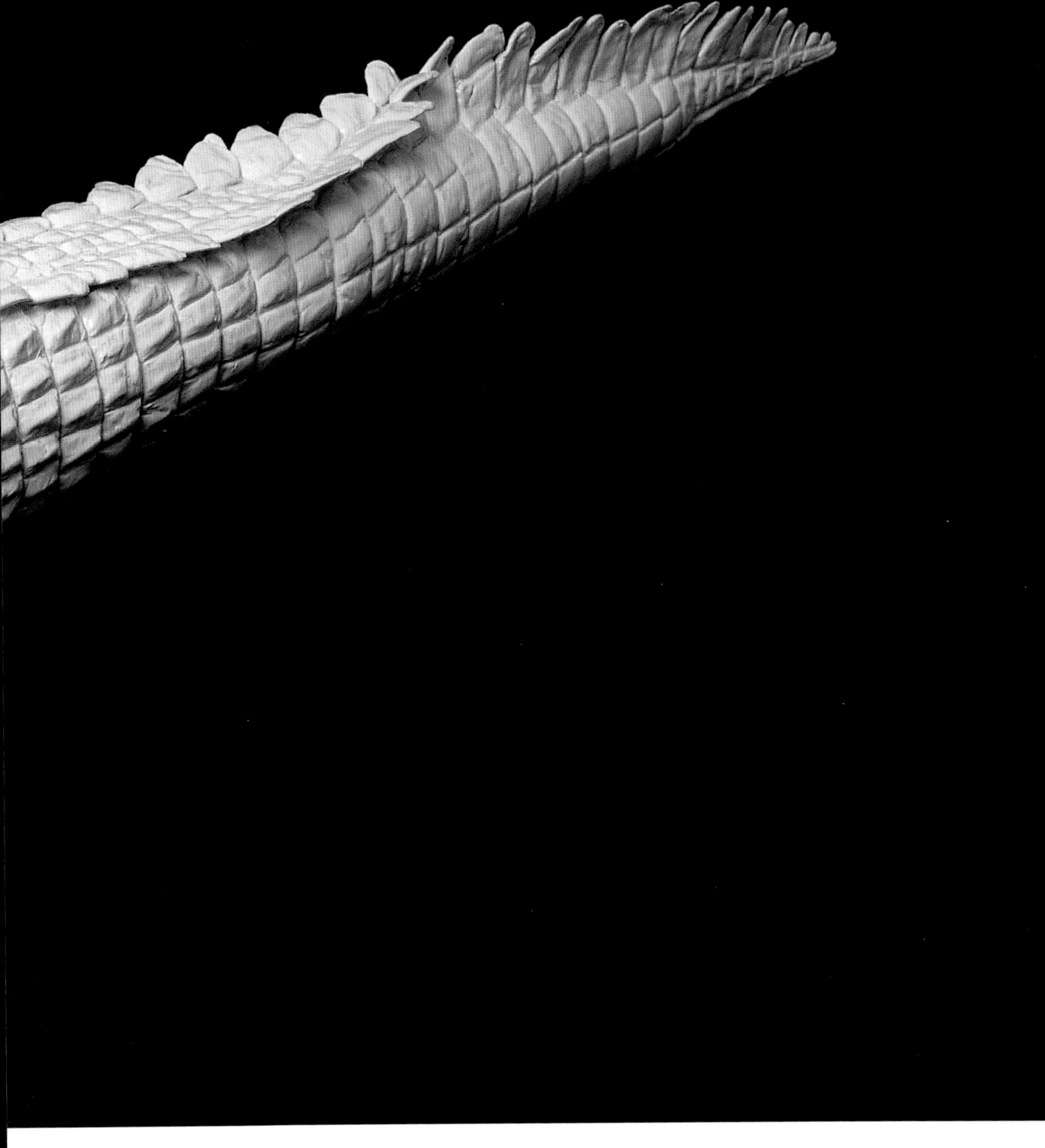

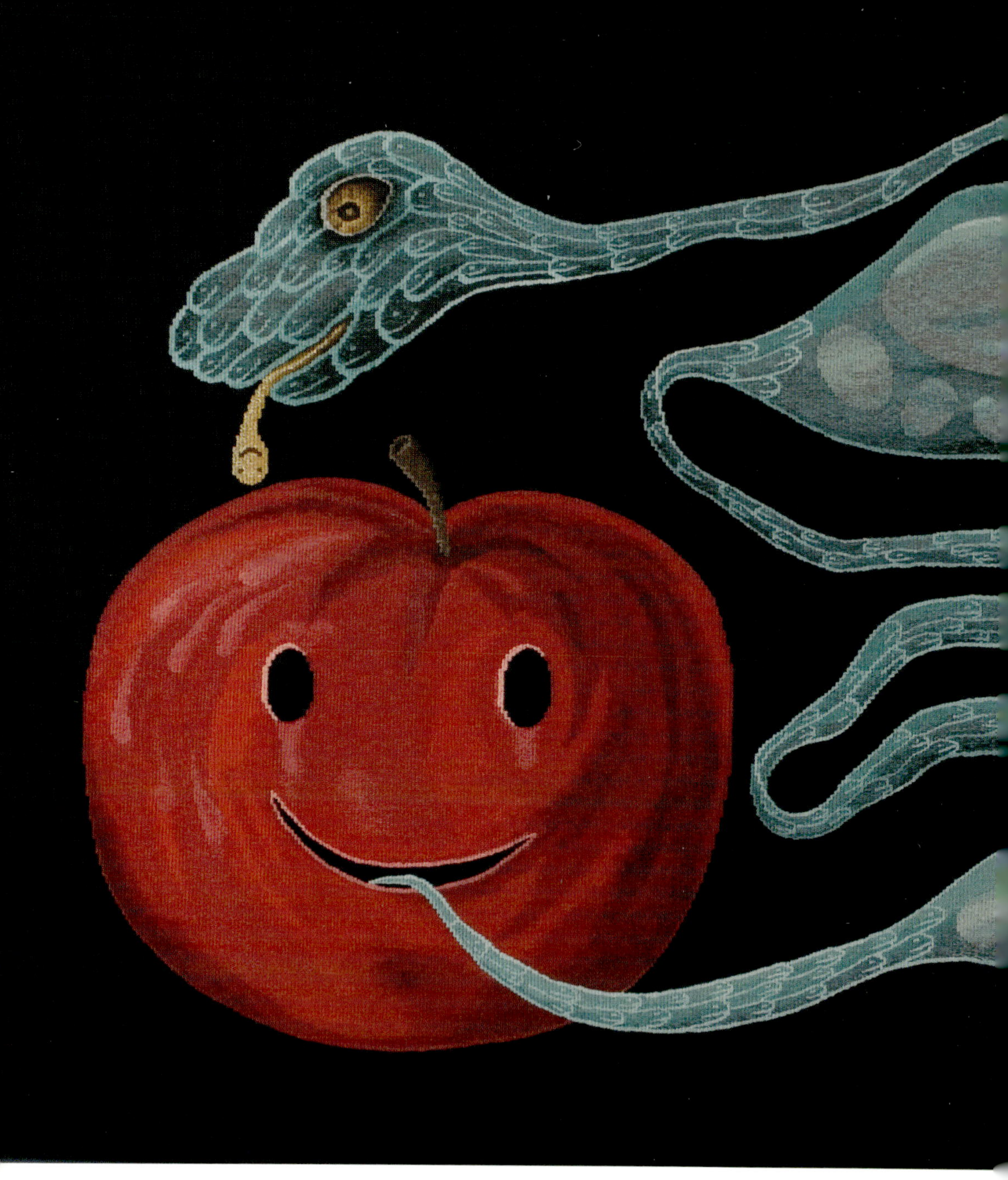

Let Me Put My Love Into You
2006

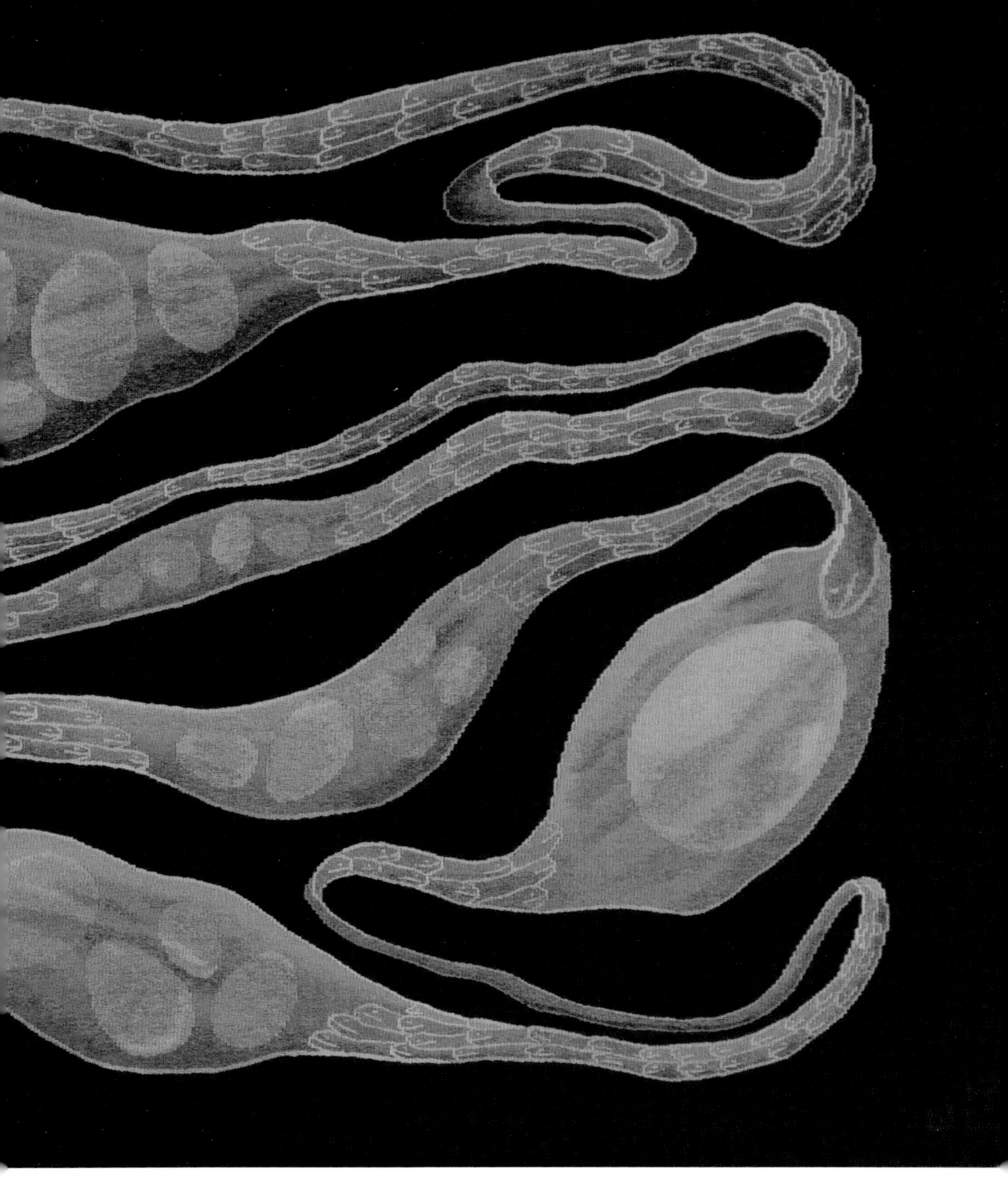

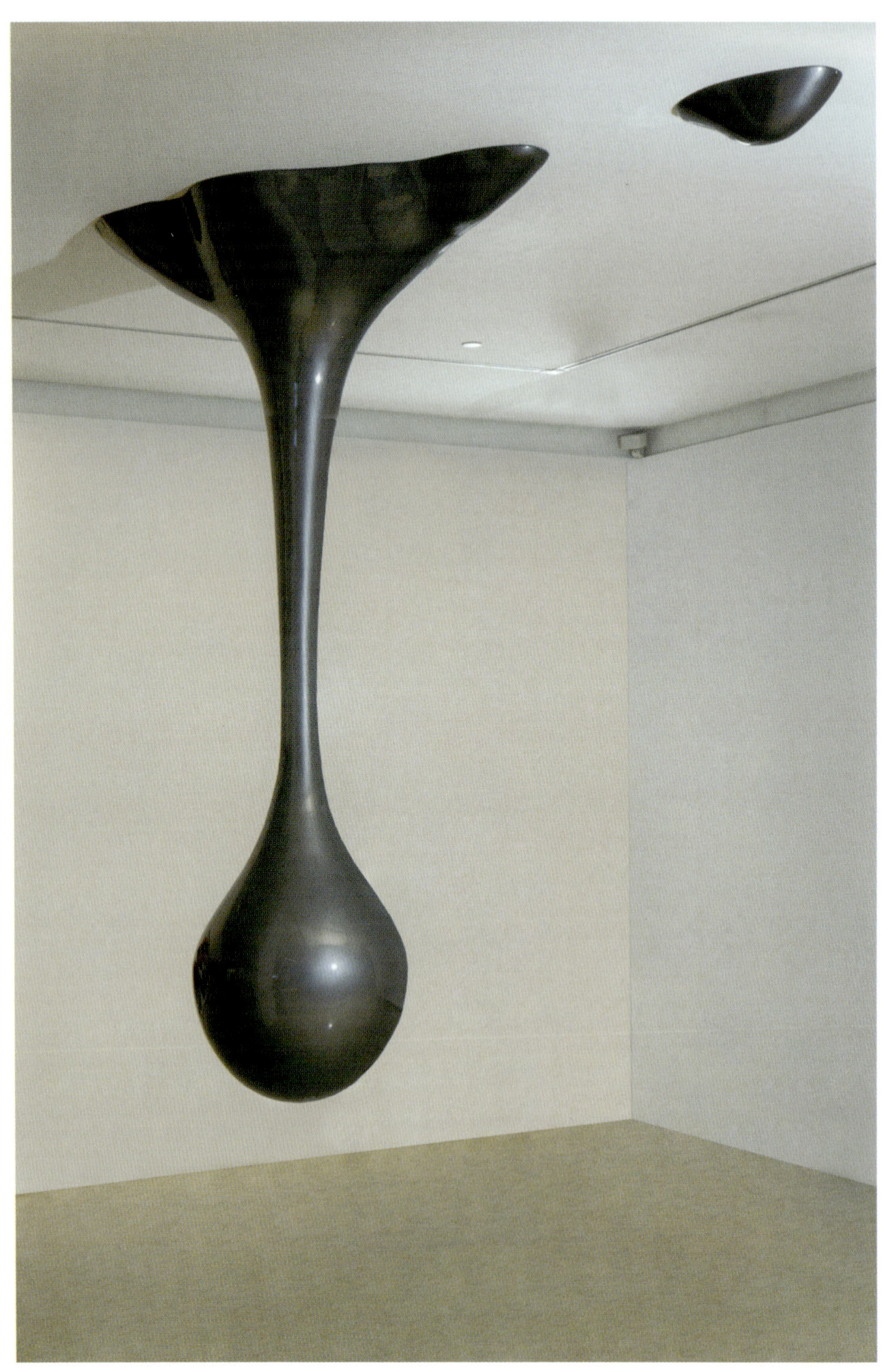

The Perfect Drip
1999

if you could hear the sound of my violin you would know how I feel
2015

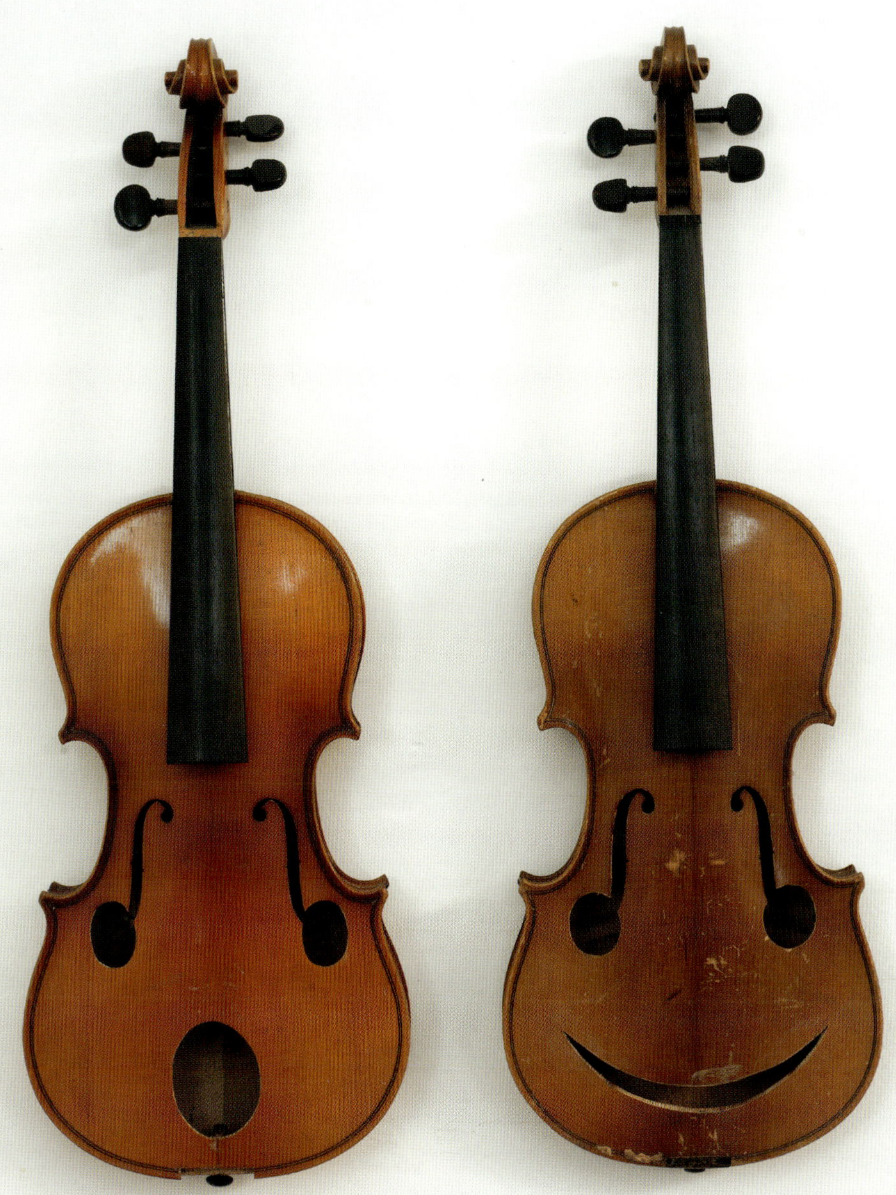

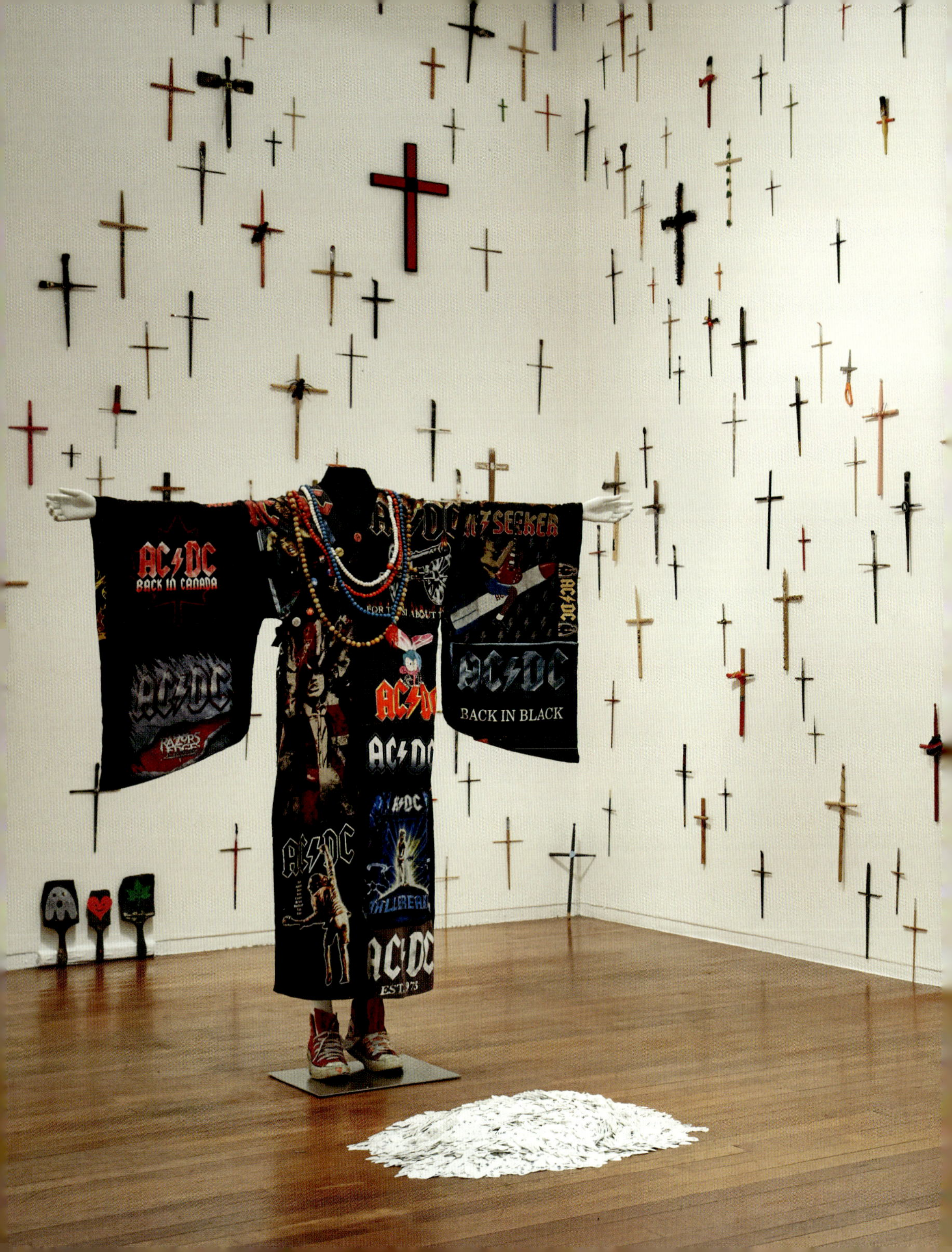
AC/DC
BACK IN CANADA
BACK IN BLACK
AC/DC
AC/DC

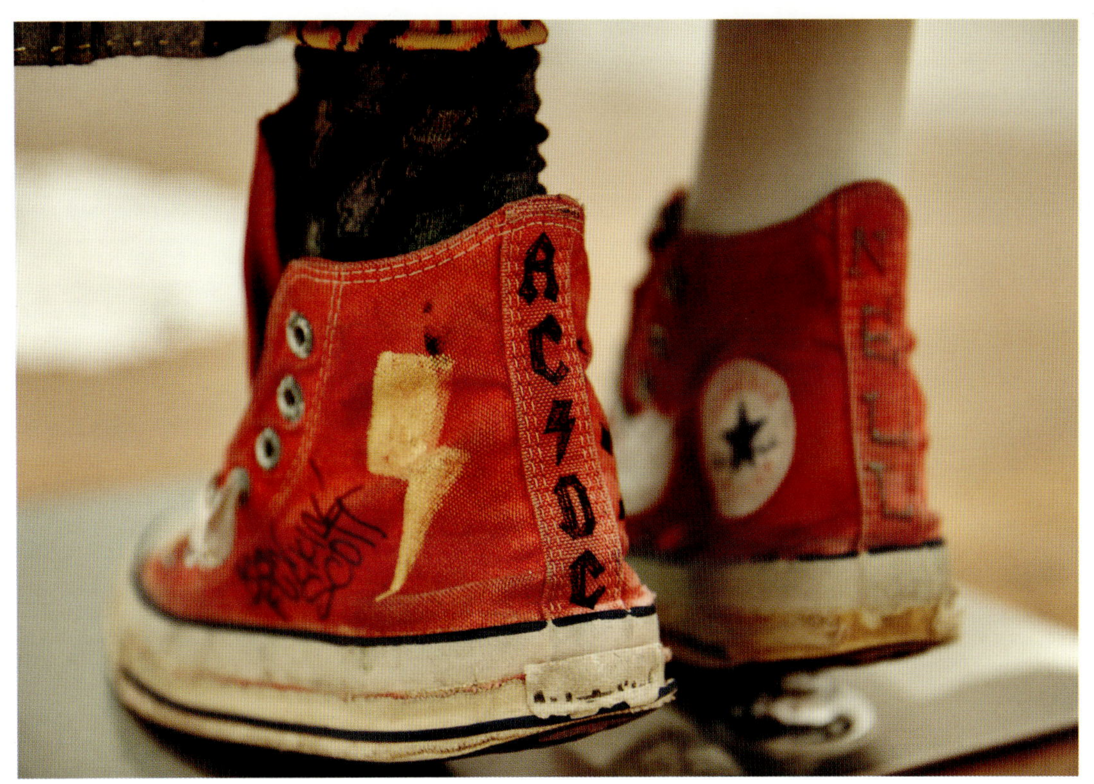

Let There Be Robe
2012

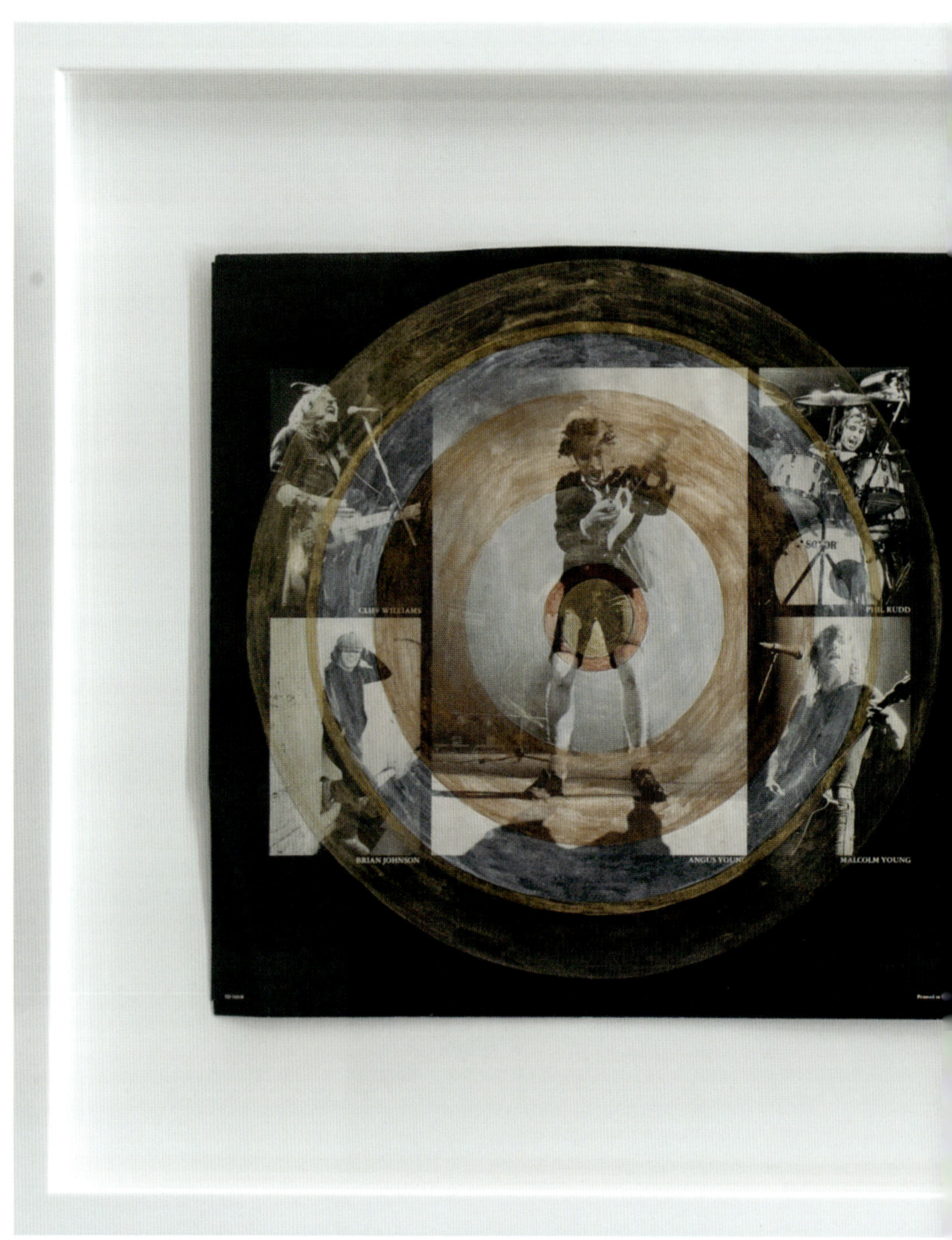

When BLACK turns GOLD 1980/2013
2013

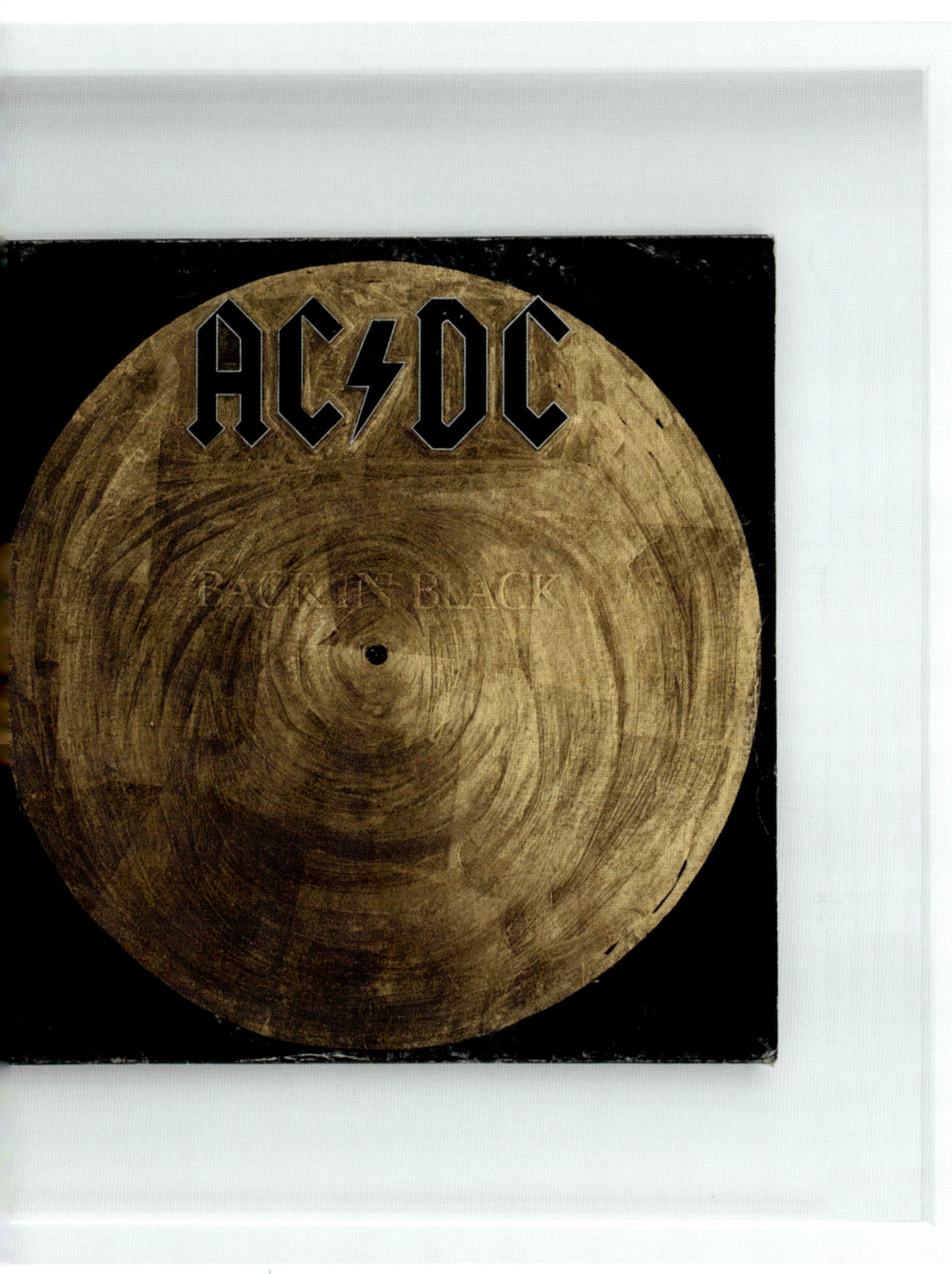
AC/DC
BACK IN BLACK

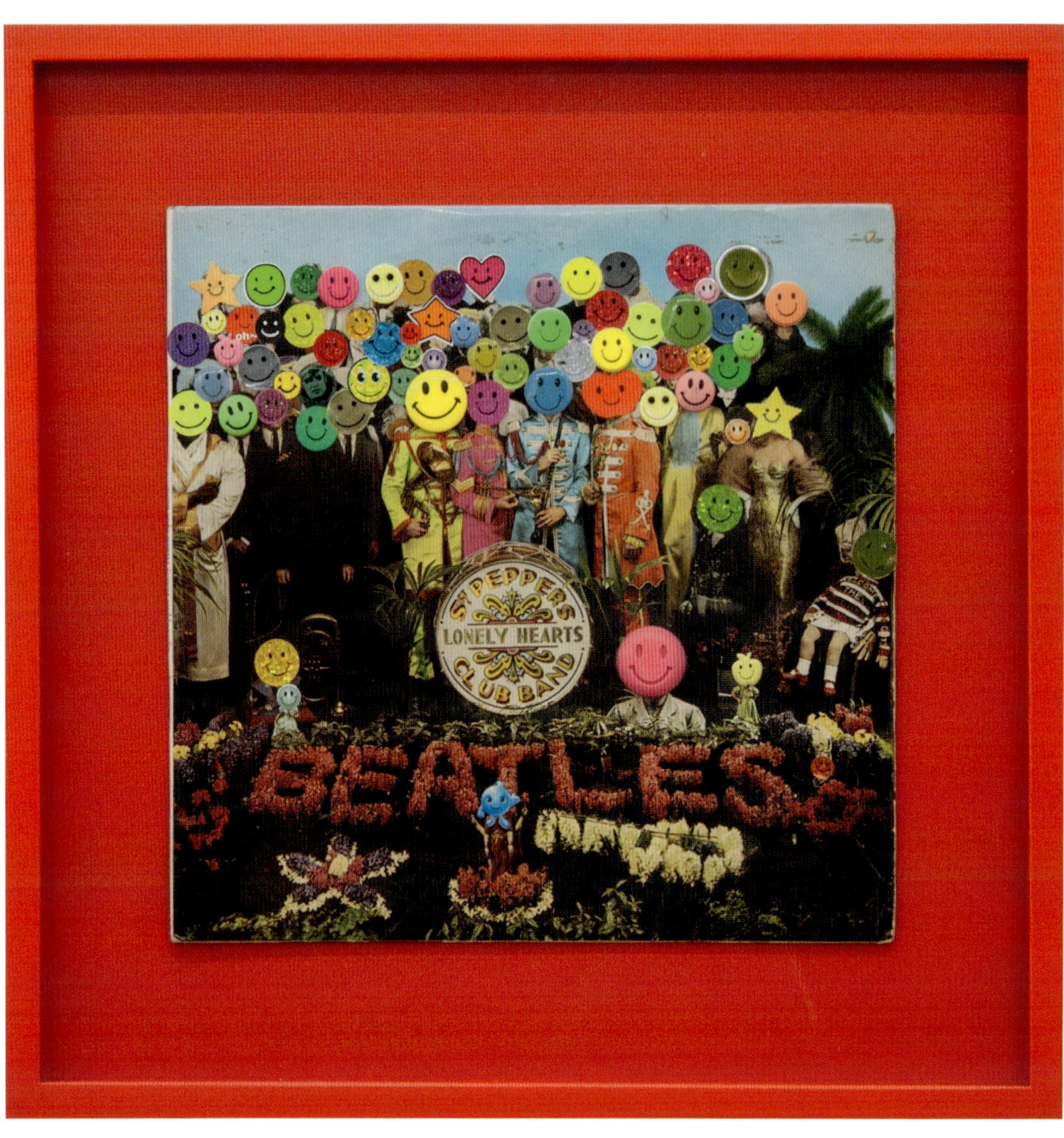

Sgt. Happy 1967/2014
2014

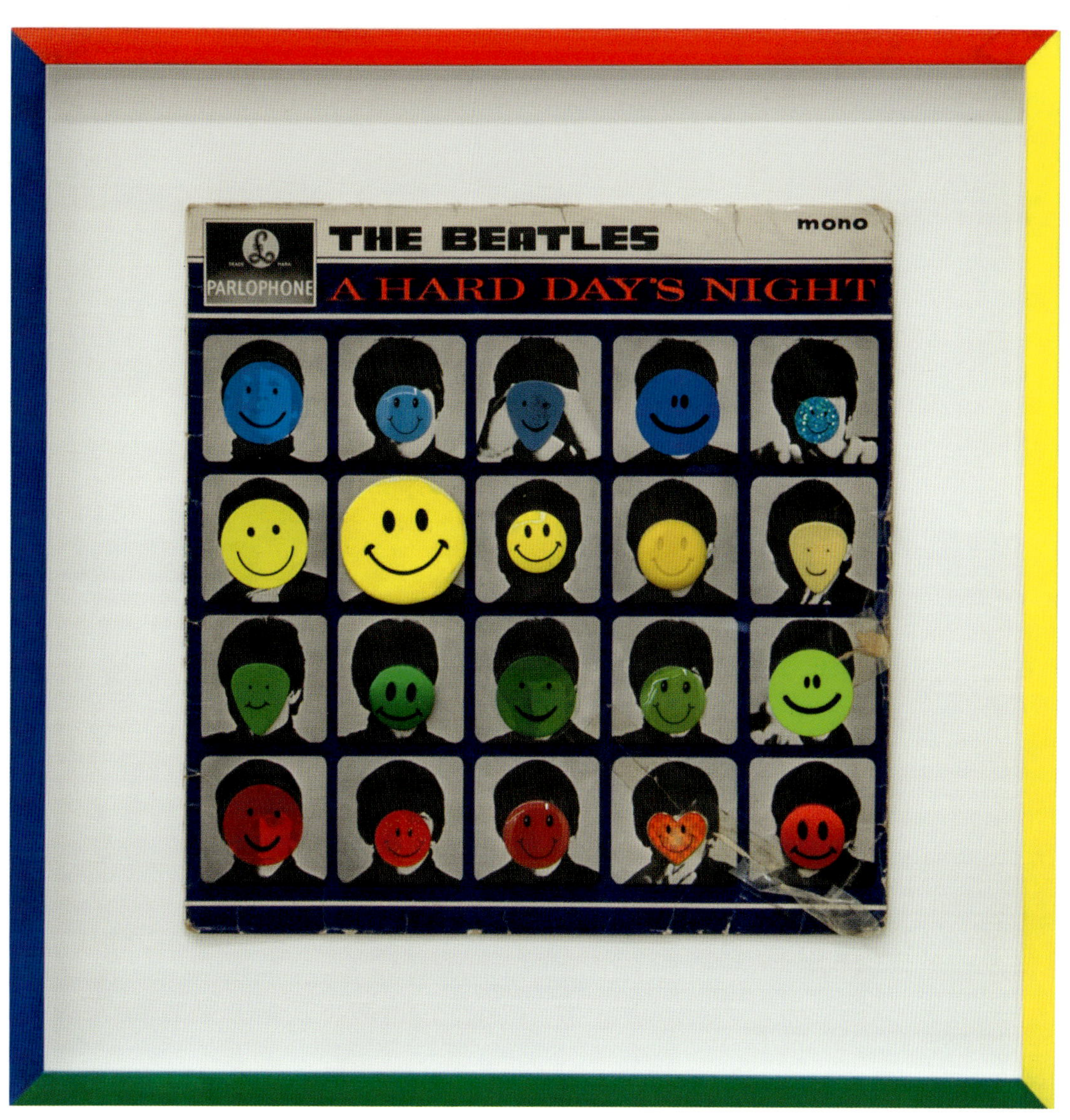

HAPPY DAY'S NIGHT 1964/2015
2015

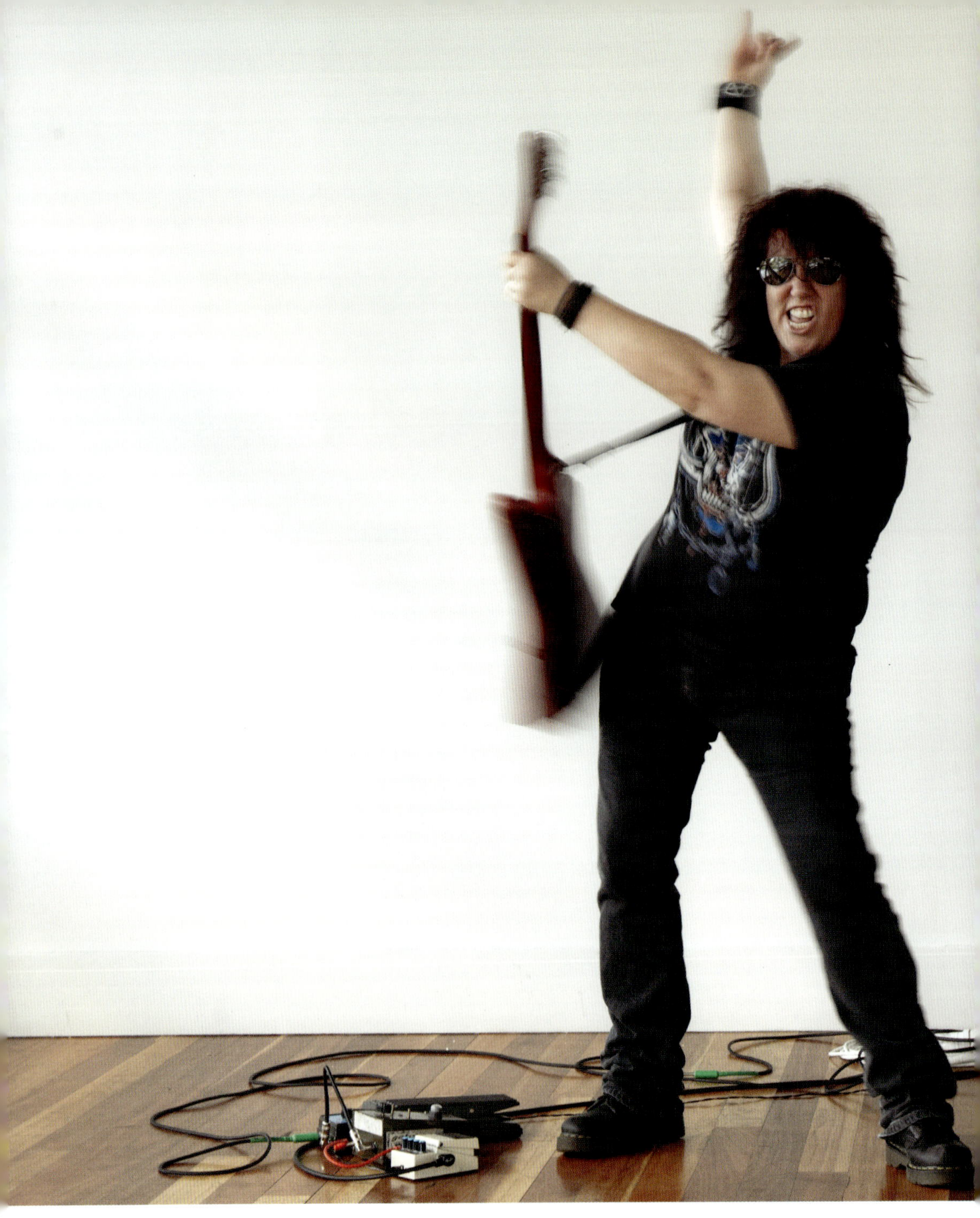

QUIET/LOUD (still), with Bec Machine from Baby Machine
2012

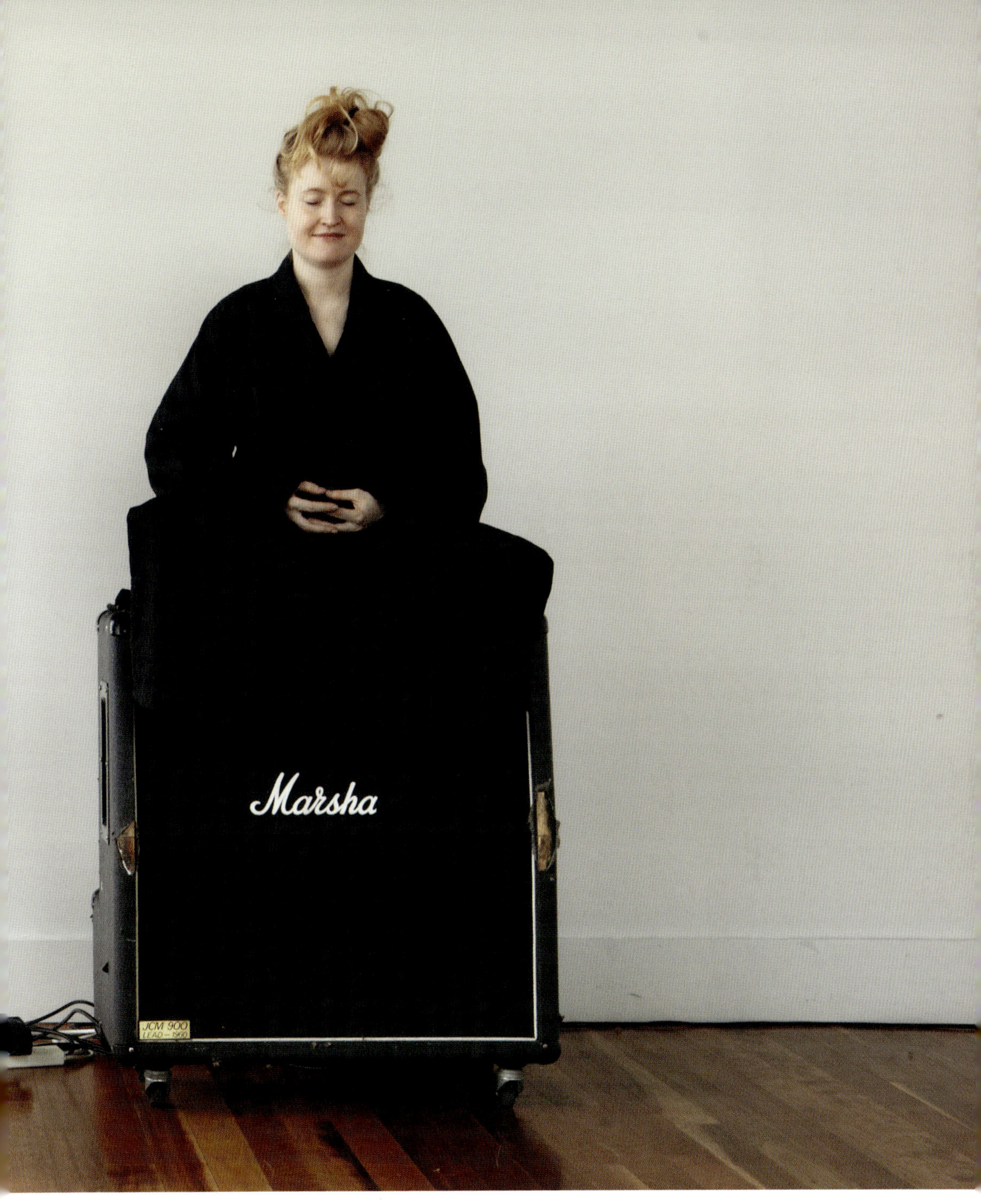
Marsha
JCM 900
LEAD – 1960

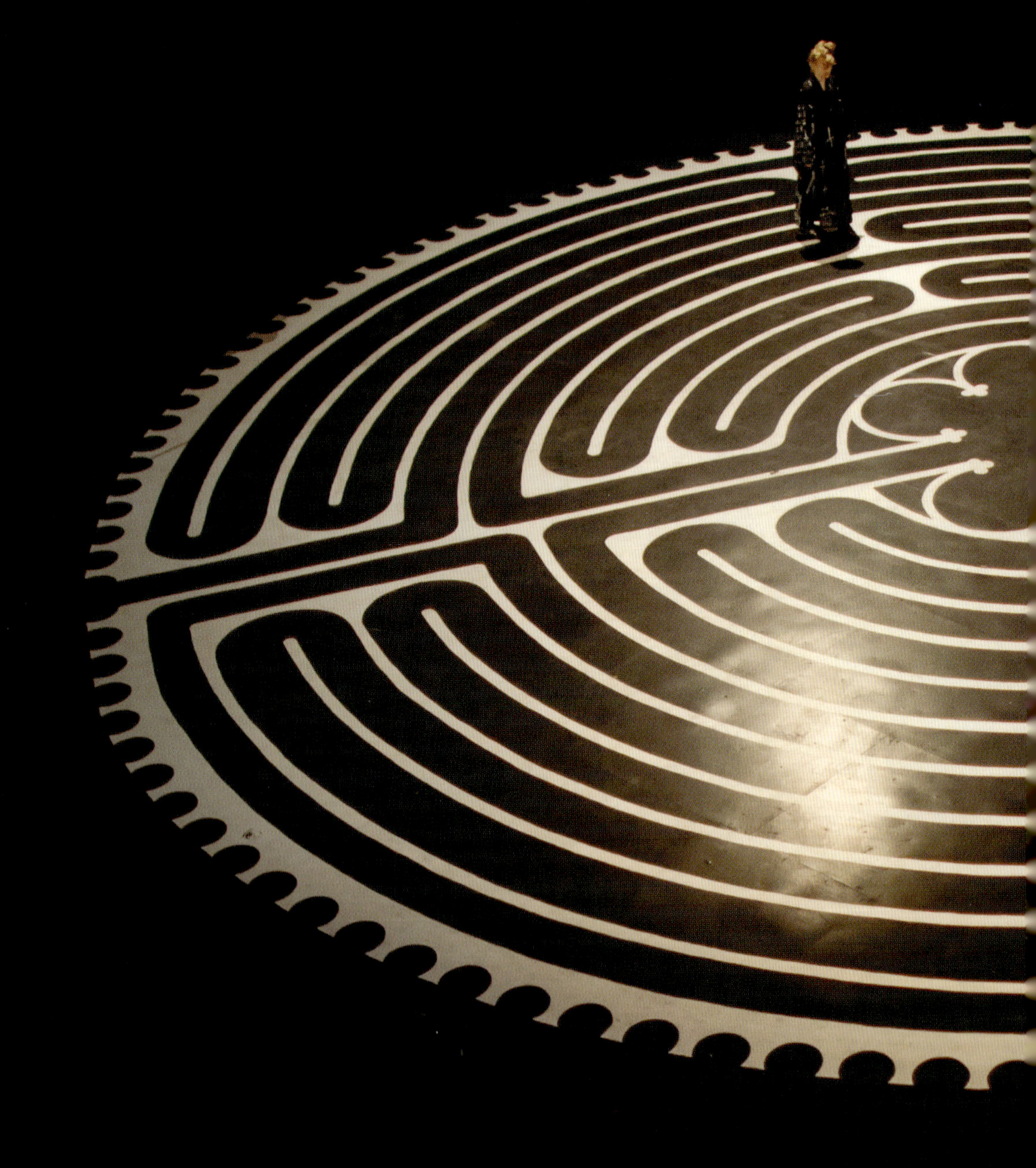

THE Labyrinth
2015

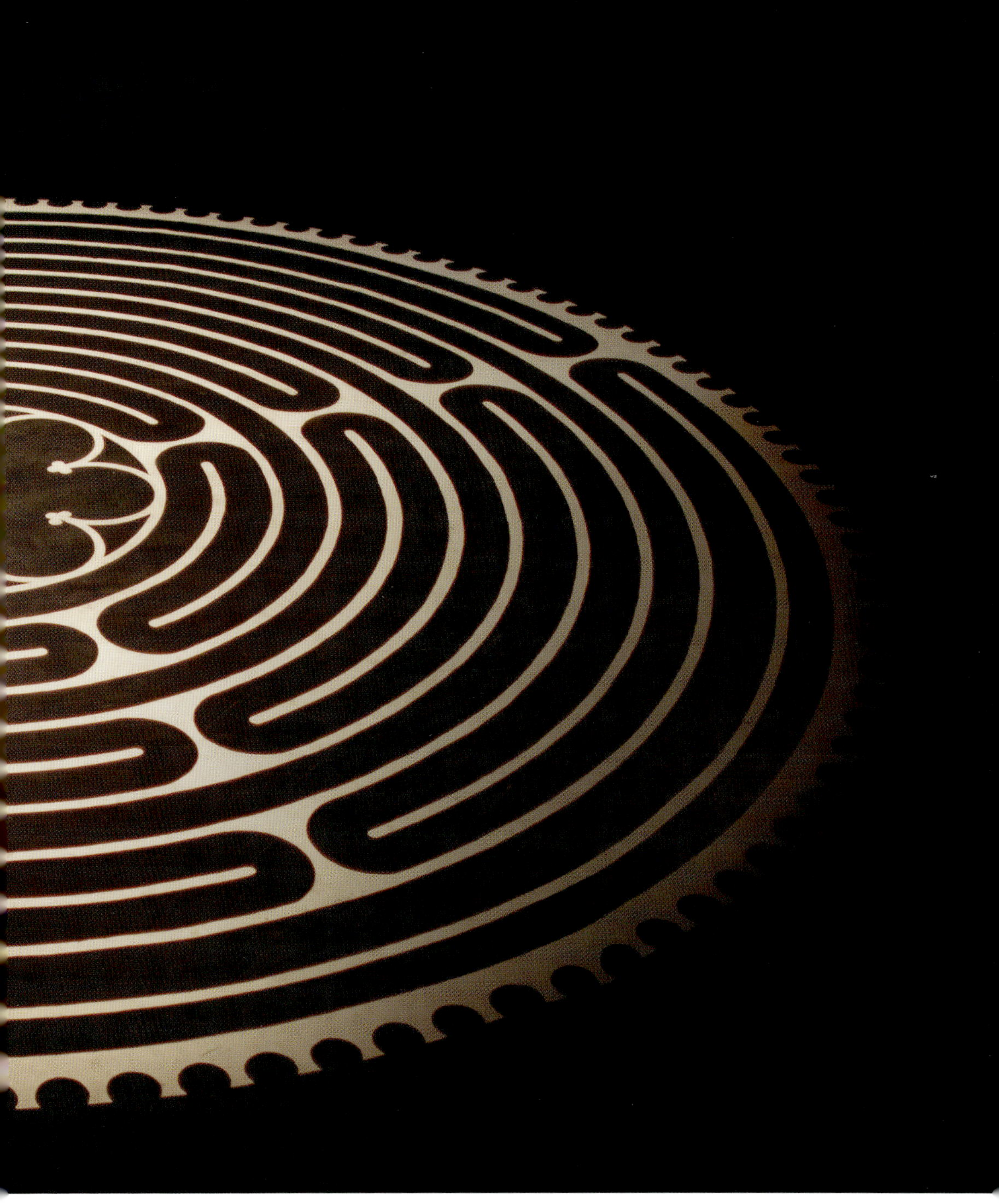

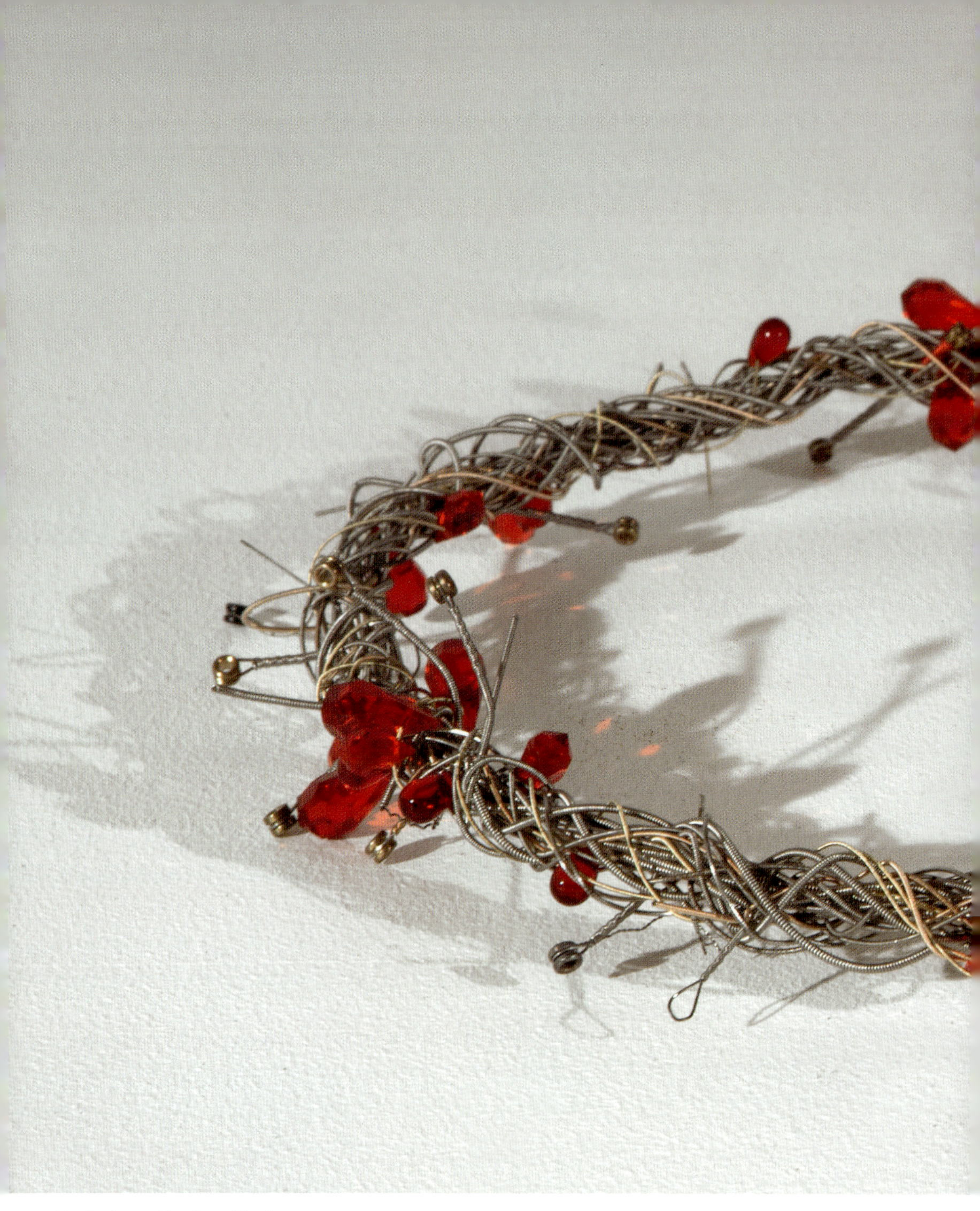

The Six Strings That Drew Blood
2012

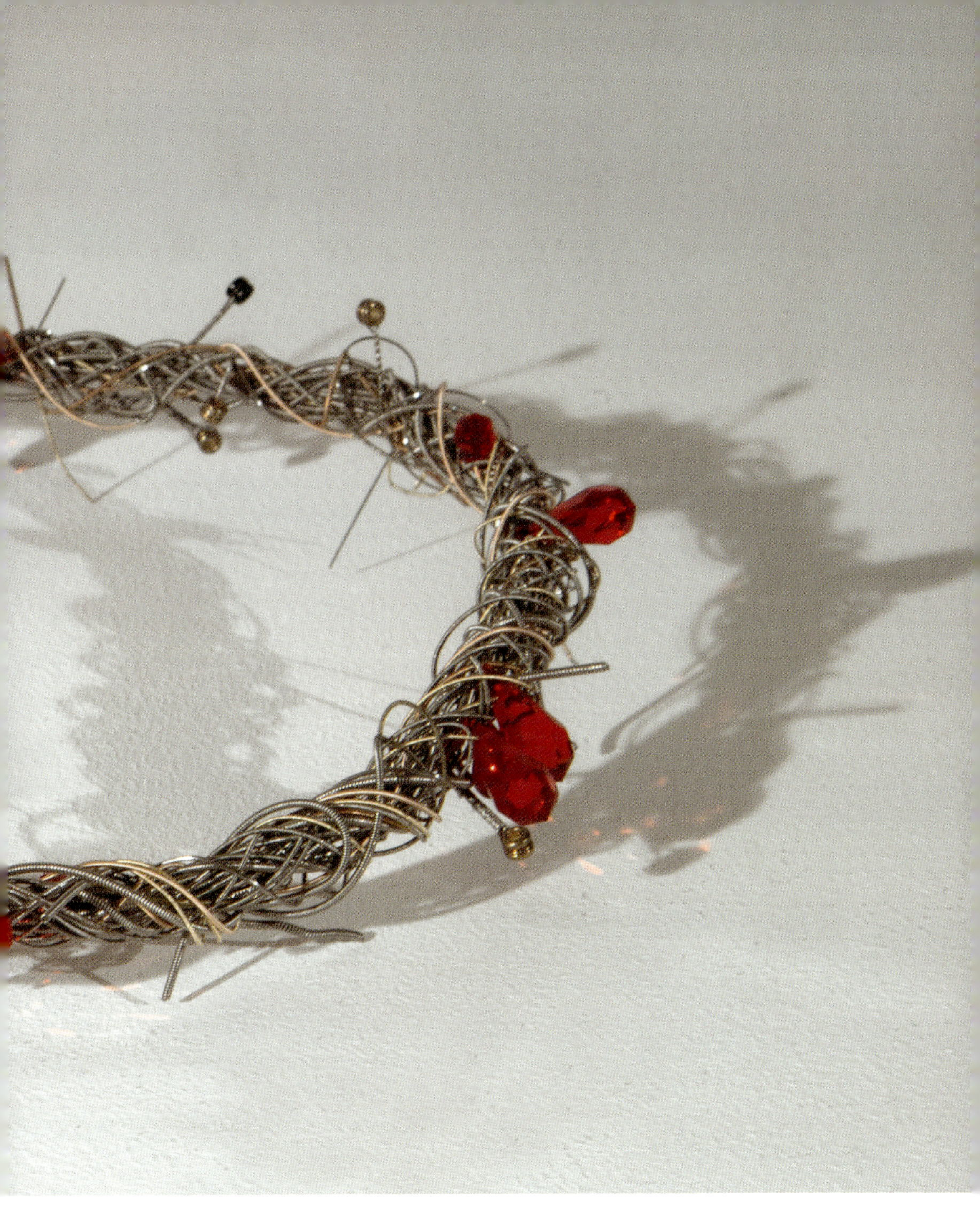

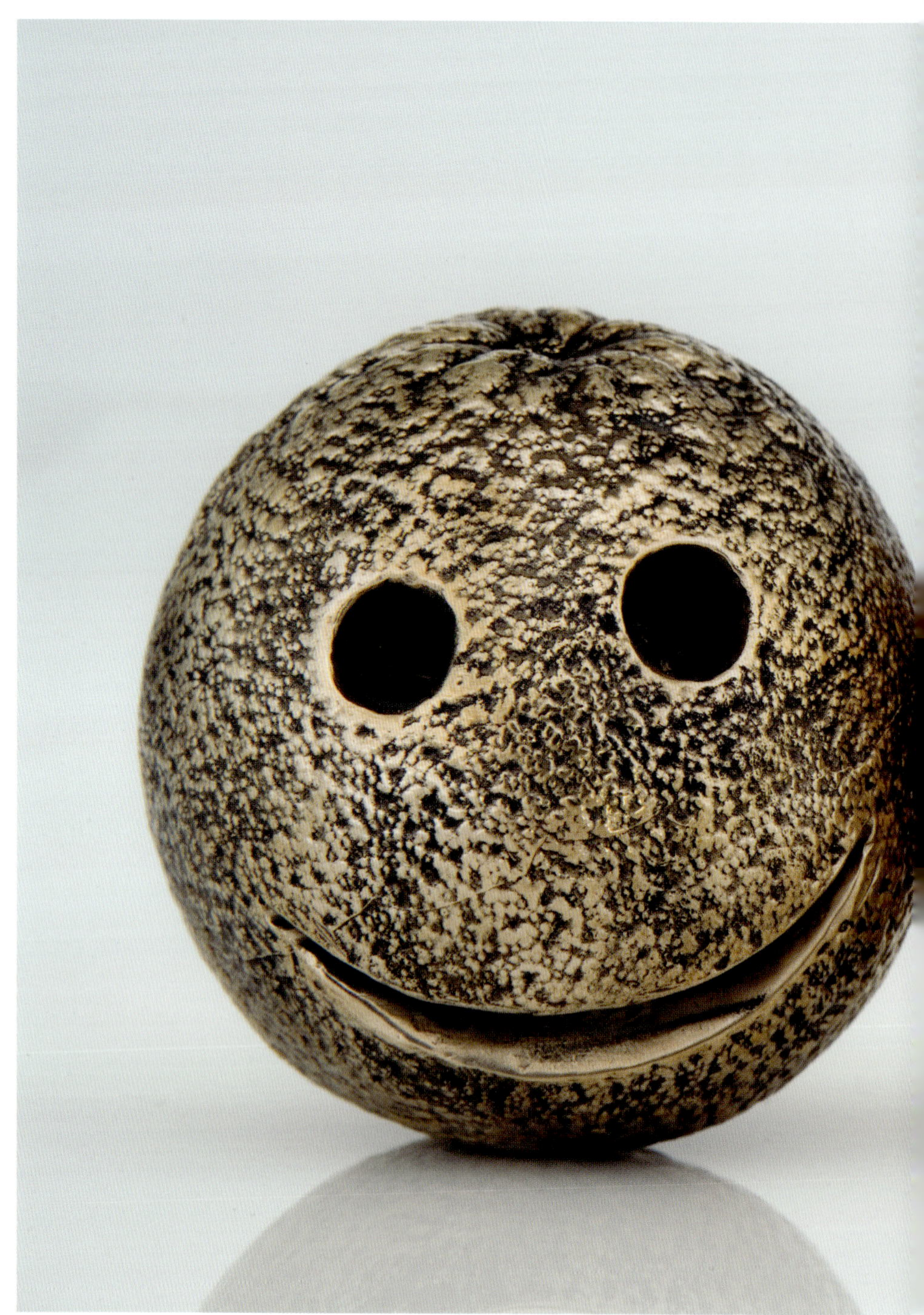

Apples and Oranges
2007

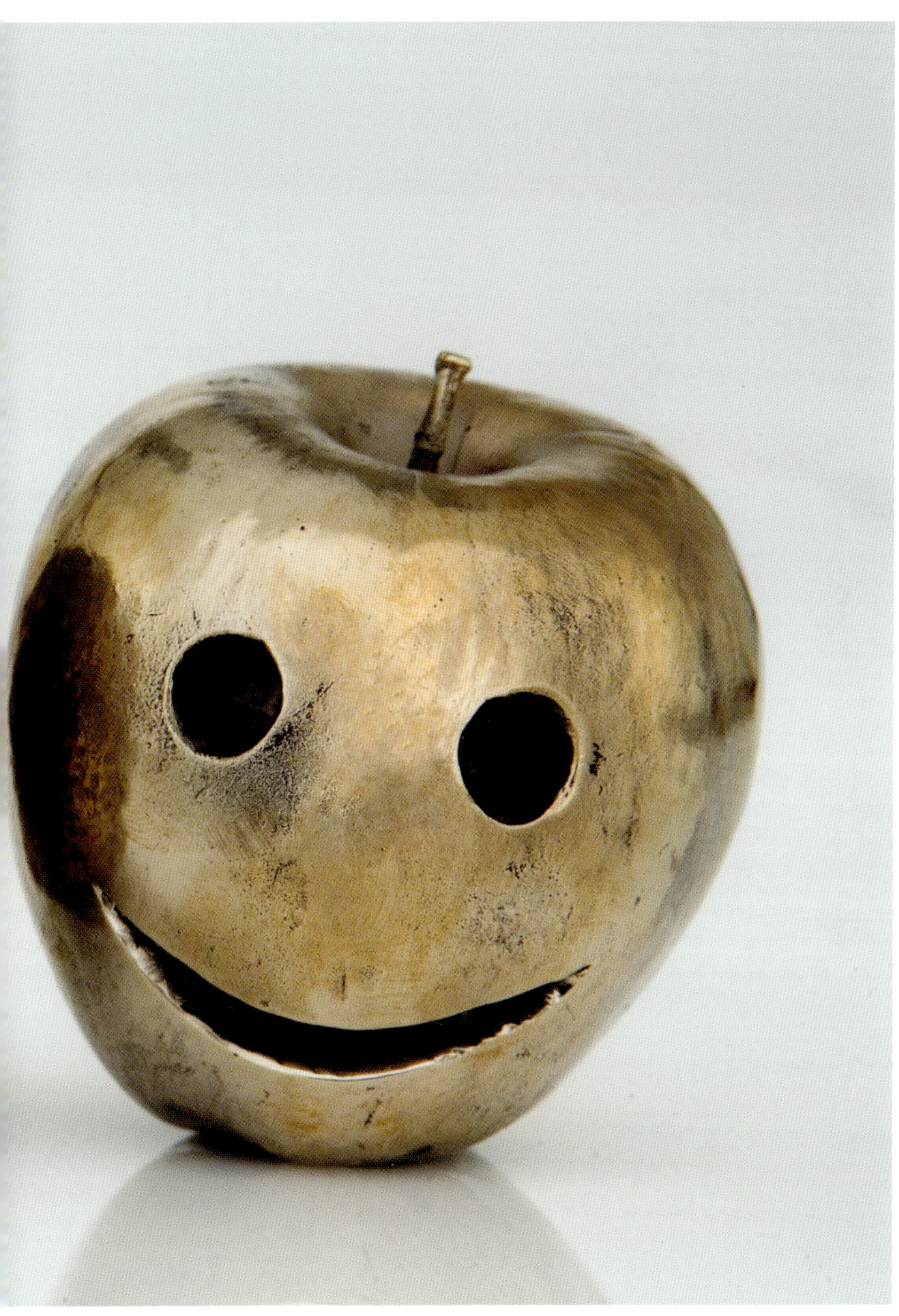

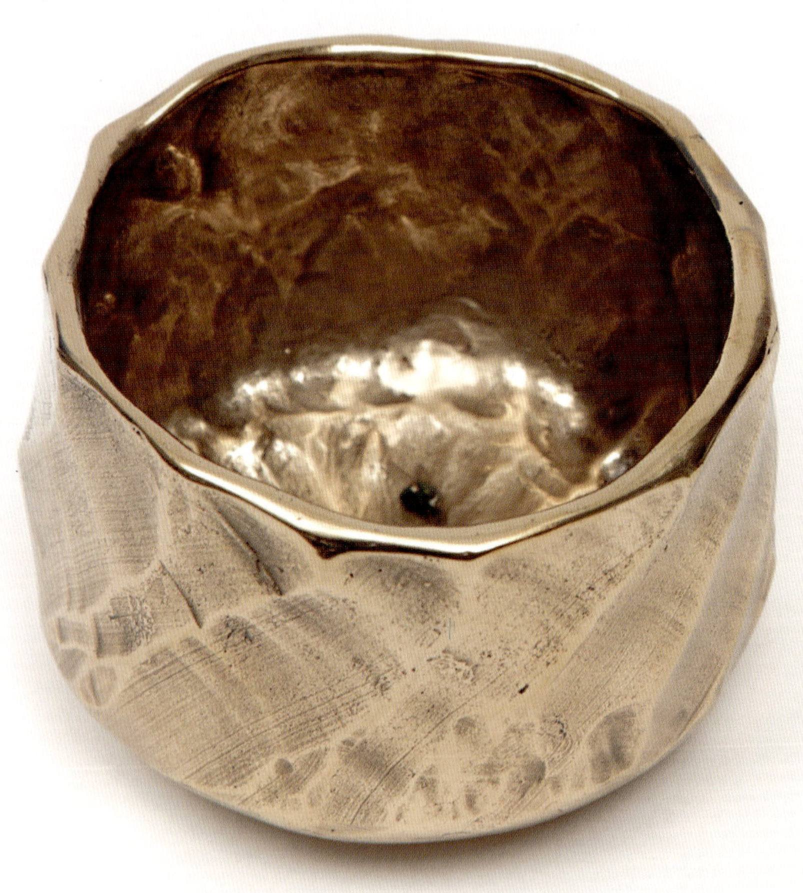

empty vessel
2015

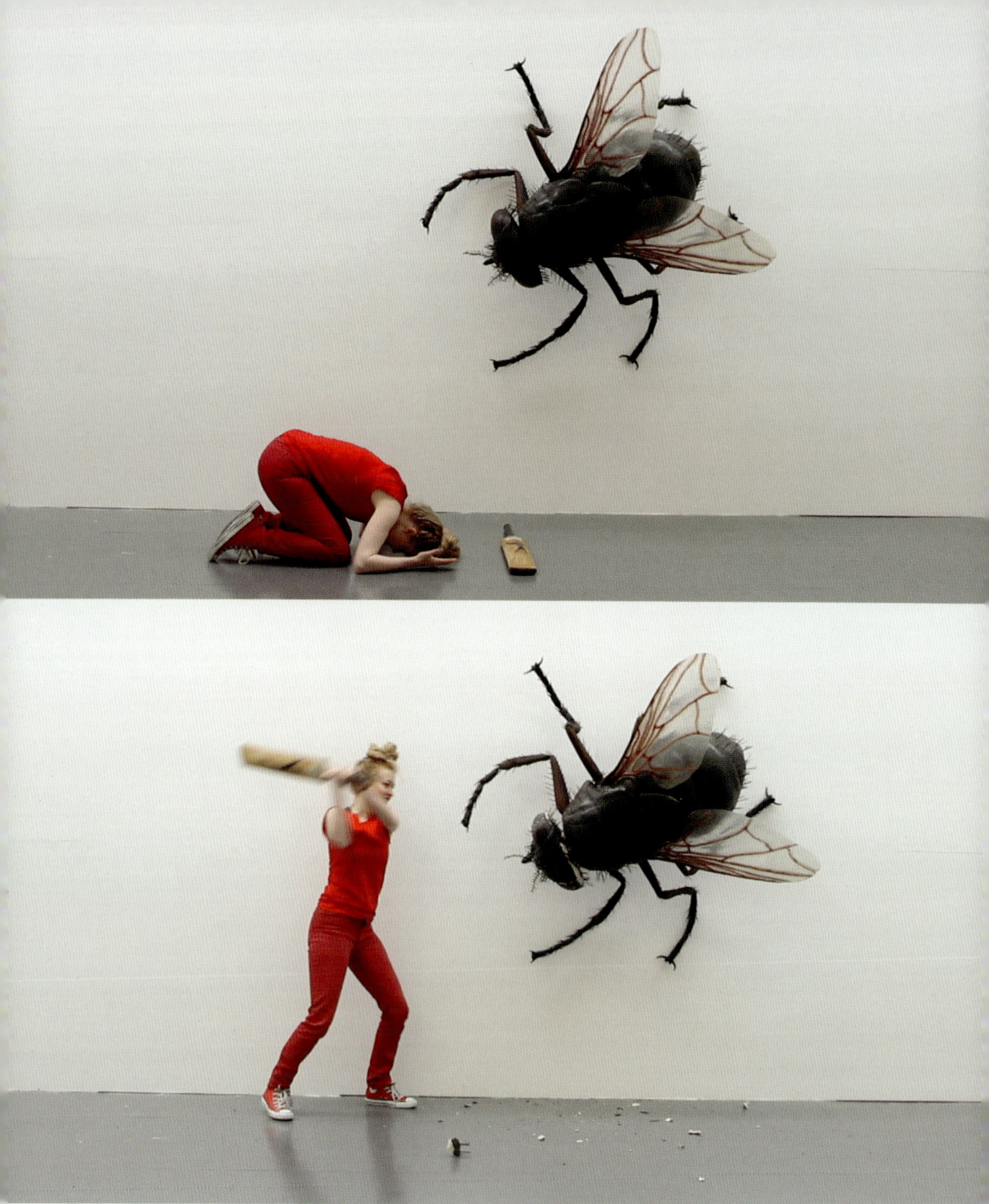

SUMMER (stills)
2012

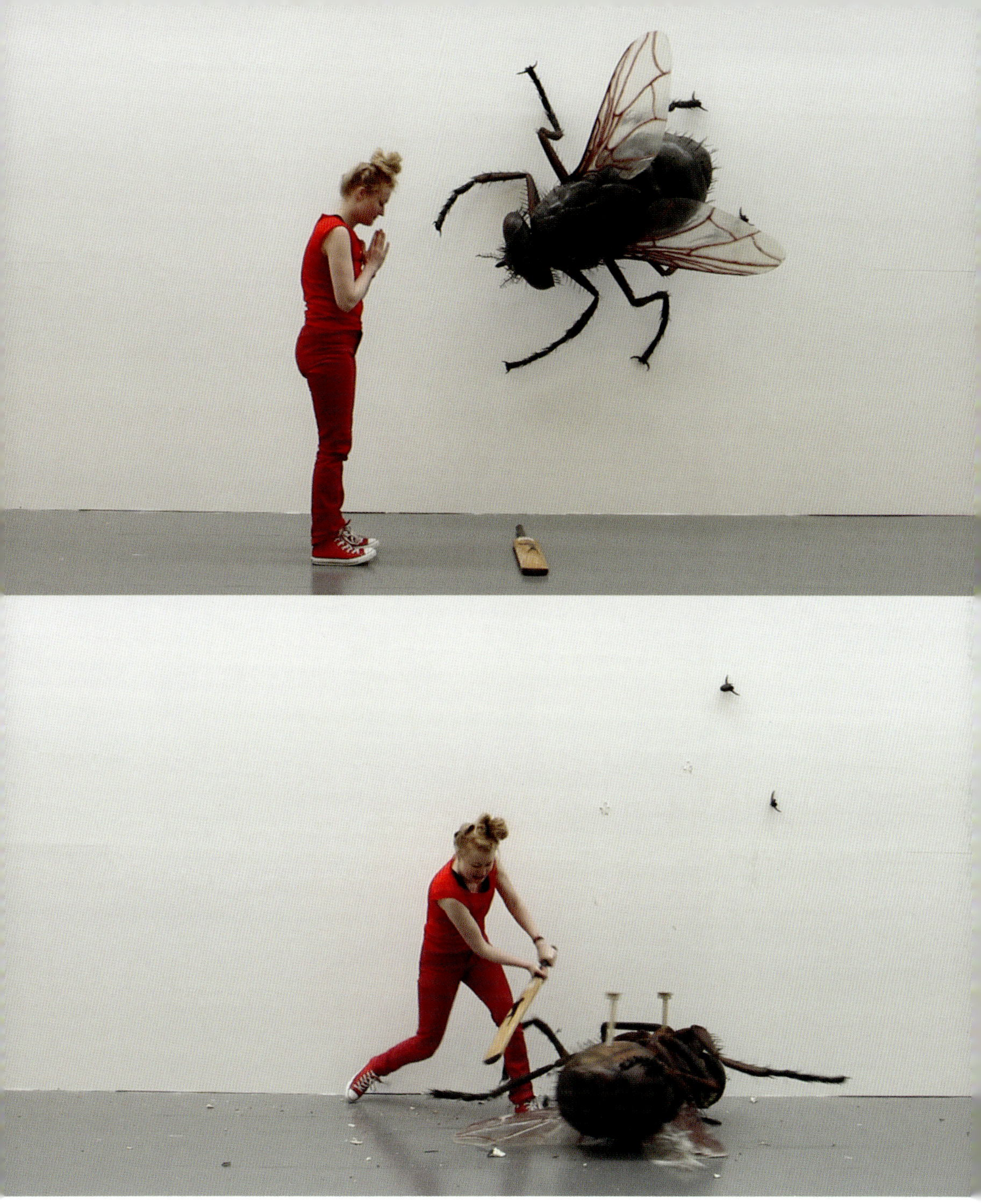

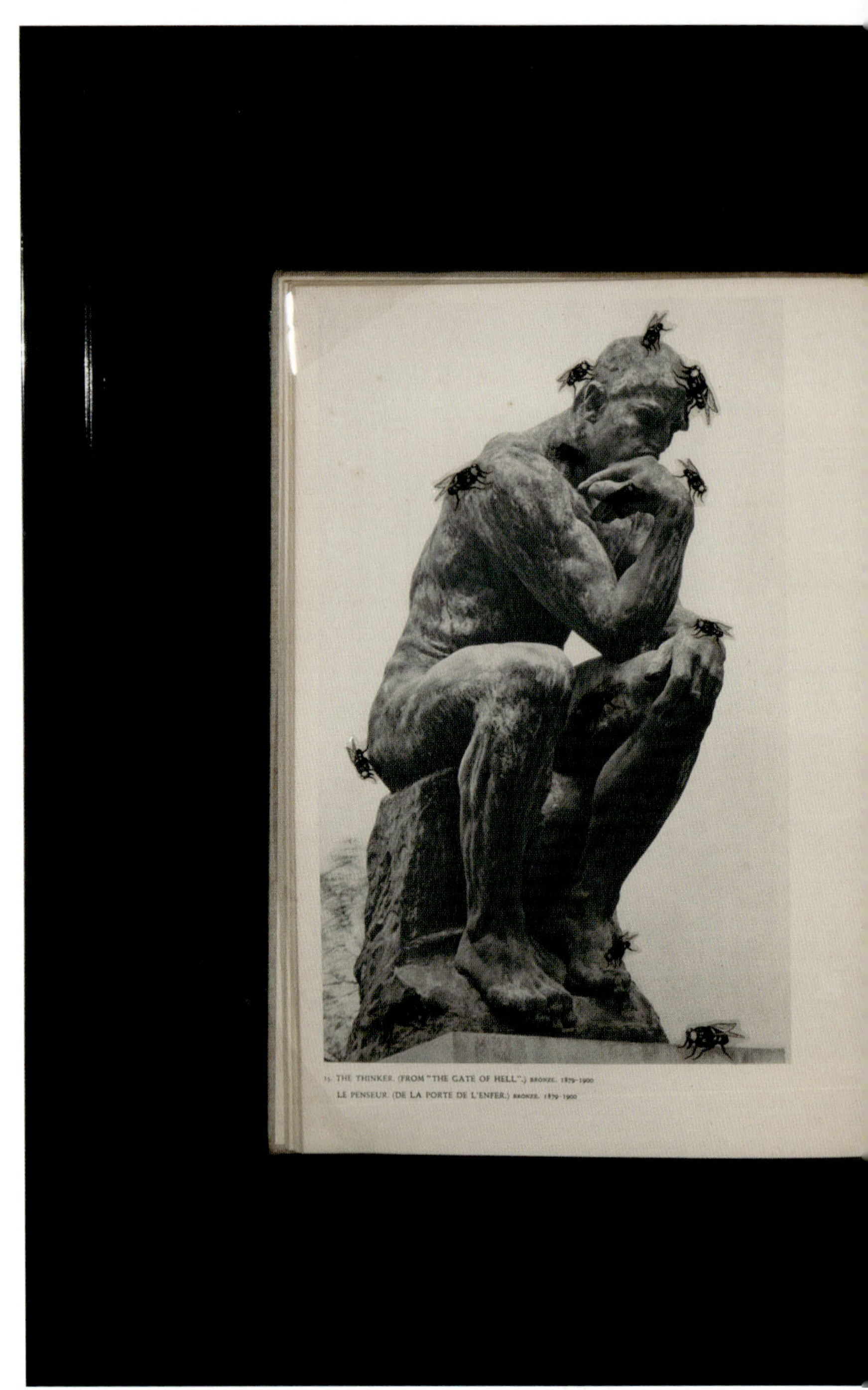

Where there are humans, you'll find flies, 1949/2013
2013

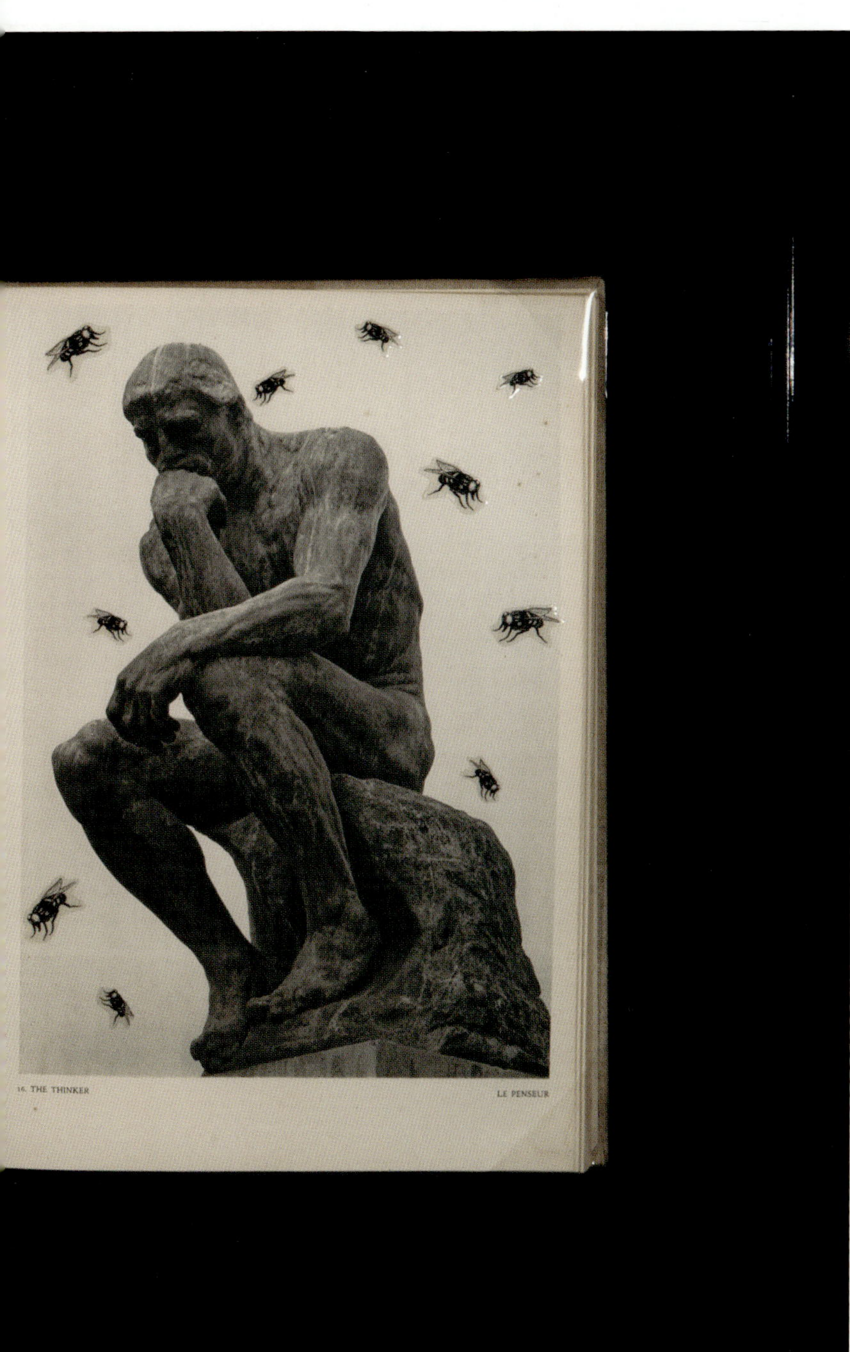
16. THE THINKER
LE PENSEUR

A Short History of Rock 'n' Roll – My Grey Album #1, 1968/2013
2013

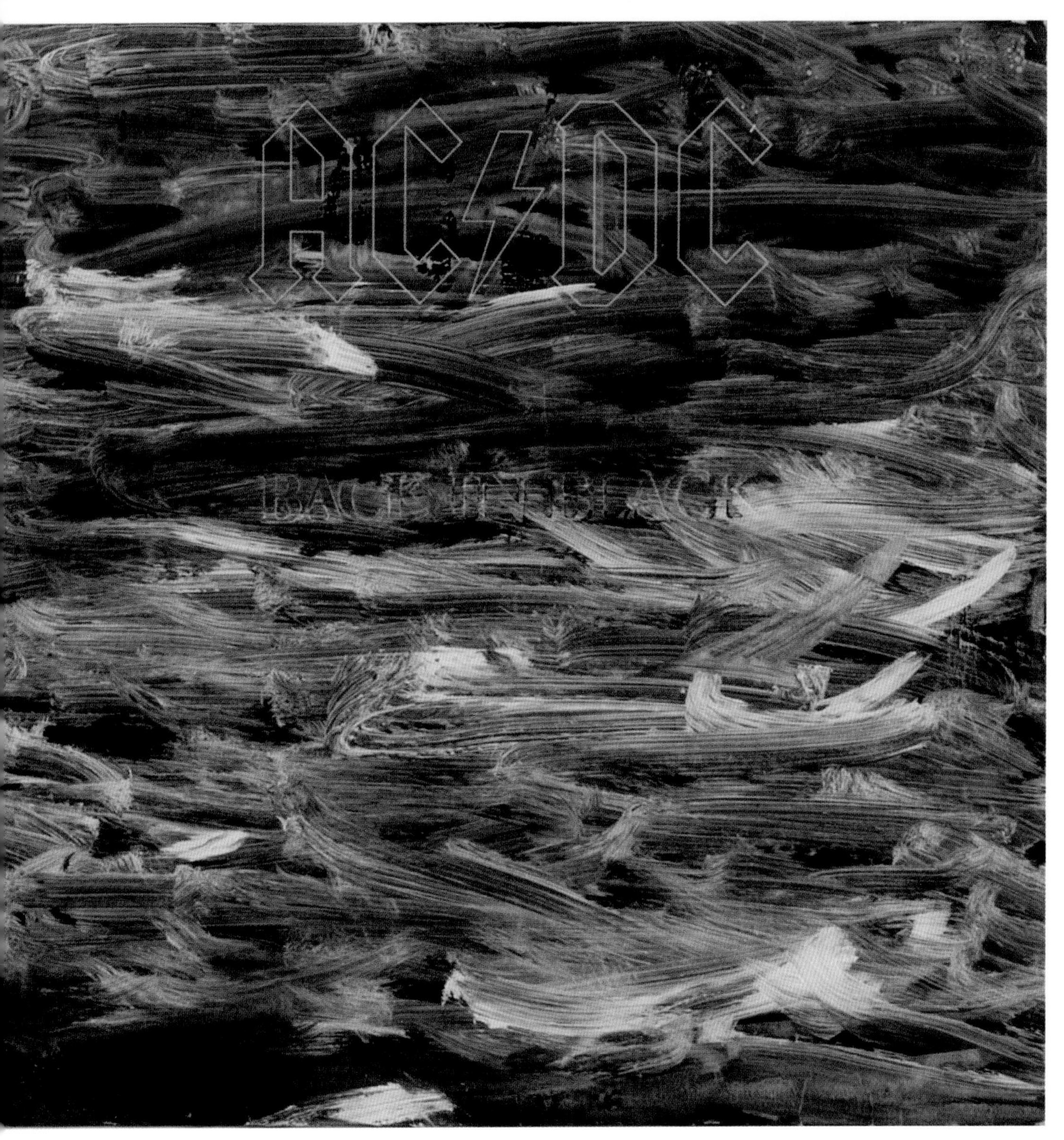
AC/DC
BACK IN BLACK

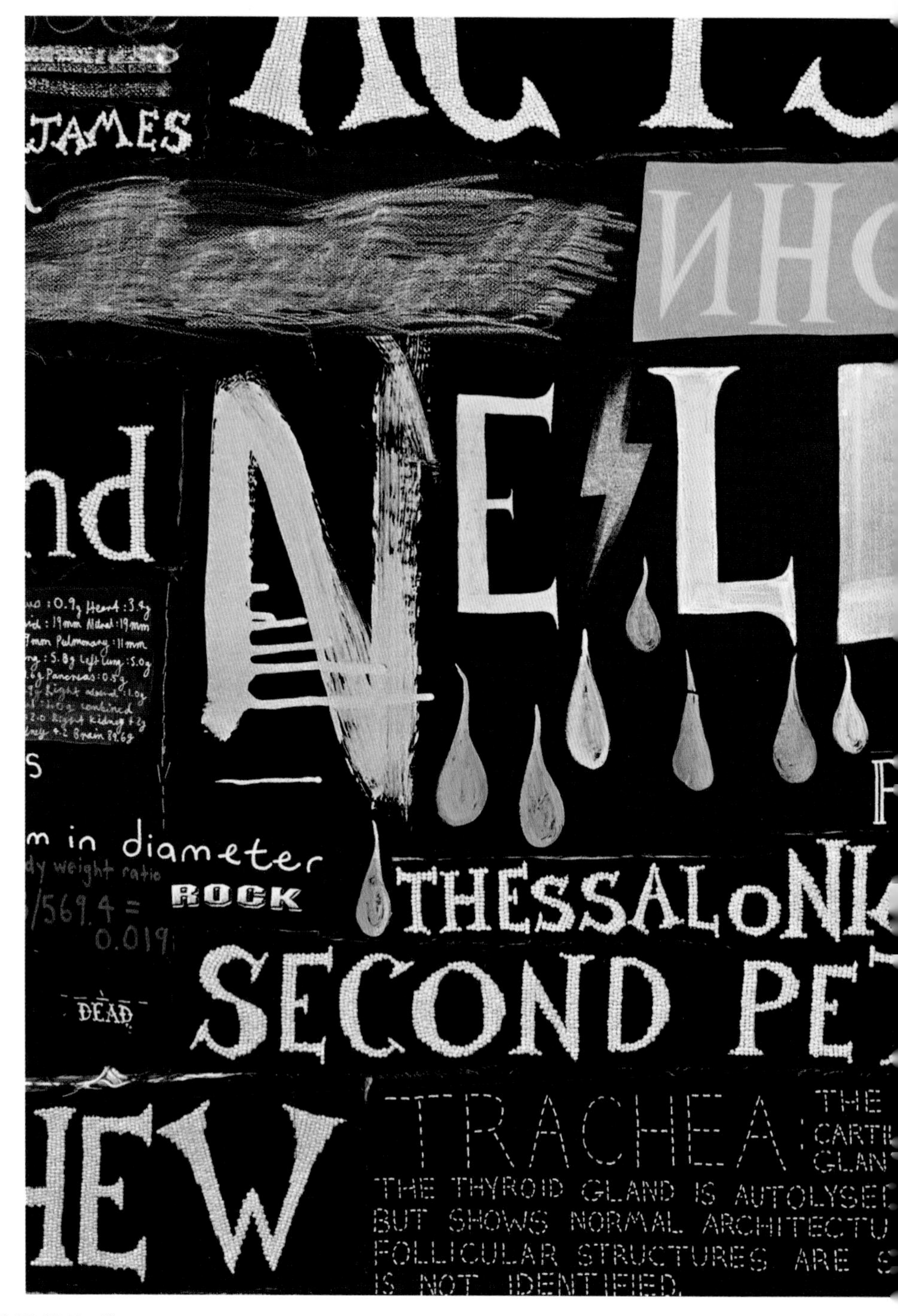

THE FIRSTBORN IS DEAD (detail)
2015

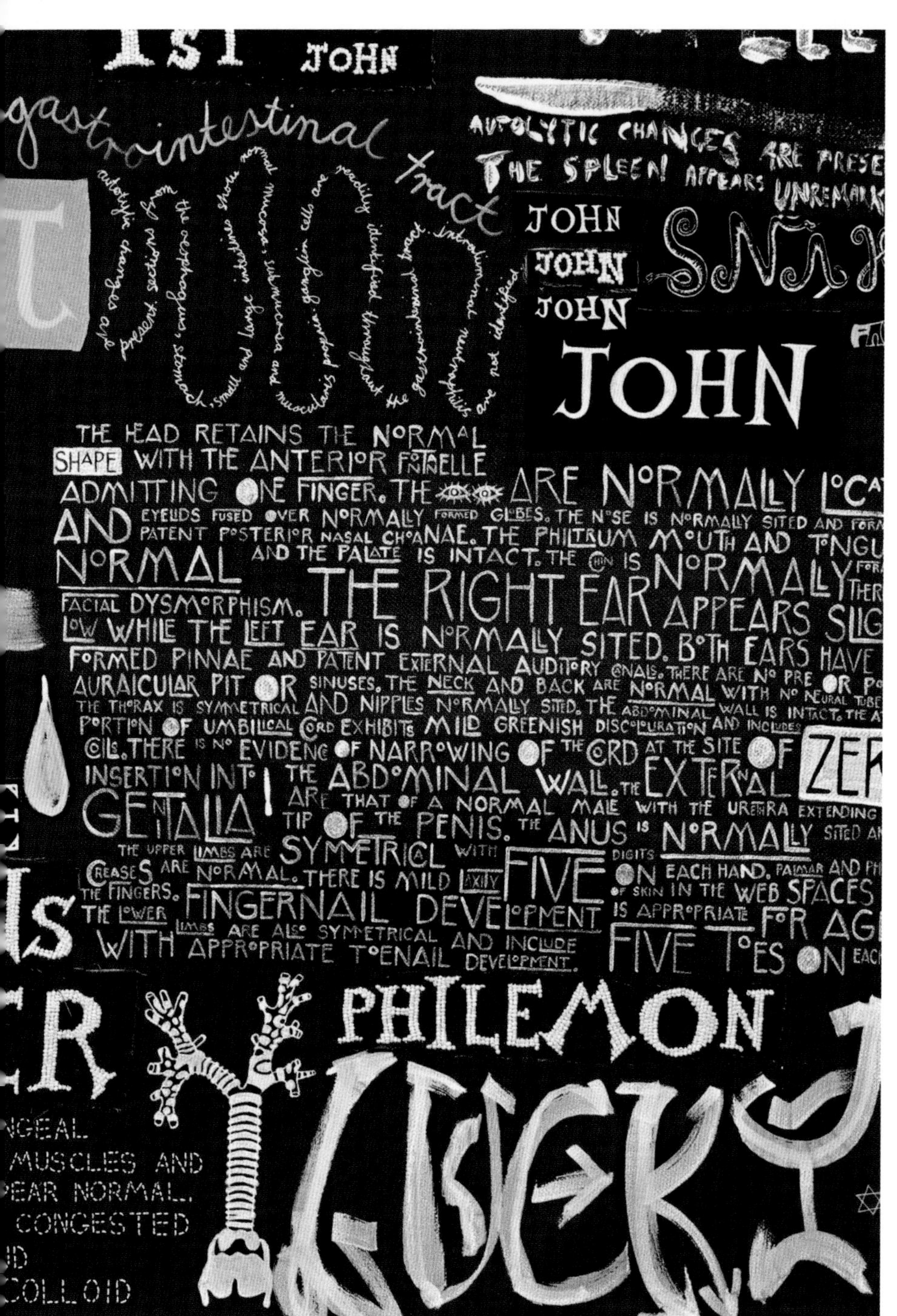
JOHN
gastrointestinal tract
autolytic changes are present. sections from the oesophagus, stomach, small and large intestine show normal mucosa, submucosa and muscularis propria. ganglion cells are readily identified throughout the gastrointestinal tract. intraluminal meconium/bile pigment are not identified
AUTOLYTIC CHANGES ARE PRESE
THE SPLEEN APPEARS UNREMARK
JOHN
JOHN
JOHN
JOHN
THE HEAD RETAINS THE NORMAL
SHAPE WITH THE ANTERIOR FONTANELLE
ADMITTING ONE FINGER. THE ARE NORMALLY LOCA
AND EYELIDS FUSED OVER NORMALLY FORMED GLOBES. THE NOSE IS NORMALLY SITED AND FORM
PATENT POSTERIOR NASAL CHOANAE. THE PHILTRUM MOUTH AND TONGU
NORMAL AND THE PALATE IS INTACT. THE CHIN IS NORMALLY
FACIAL DYSMORPHISM. THE RIGHT EAR APPEARS SLIG
LOW WHILE THE LEFT EAR IS NORMALLY SITED. BOTH EARS HAVE
FORMED PINNAE AND PATENT EXTERNAL AUDITORY CANALS. THERE ARE NO PRE OR PO
AURAICULAR PIT OR SINUSES. THE NECK AND BACK ARE NORMAL WITH NO NEURAL TUBE
THE THORAX IS SYMMETRICAL AND NIPPLES NORMALLY SITED. THE ABDOMINAL WALL IS INTACT. THE A
PORTION OF UMBILICAL CORD EXHIBITS MILD GREENISH DISCOLOURATION AND INCLUDES
COILS. THERE IS NO EVIDENCE OF NARROWING OF THE CORD AT THE SITE OF
INSERTION INTO THE ABDOMINAL WALL. THE EXTERNAL
GENITALIA ARE THAT OF A NORMAL MALE WITH THE URETHRA EXTENDING
TIP OF THE PENIS. THE ANUS IS NORMALLY SITED AN
THE UPPER LIMBS ARE SYMMETRICAL WITH FIVE DIGITS ON EACH HAND. PALMAR AND PH
CREASES ARE NORMAL. THERE IS MILD LAXITY OF SKIN IN THE WEB SPACES
THE FINGERS. FINGERNAIL DEVELOPMENT IS APPROPRIATE FOR AG
THE LOWER LIMBS ARE ALSO SYMMETRICAL
WITH APPROPRIATE TOENAIL AND INCLUDE DEVELOPMENT. FIVE TOES ON EACH
PHILEMON
NGEAL
MUSCLES AND
EAR NORMAL.
CONGESTED
D
COLLOID

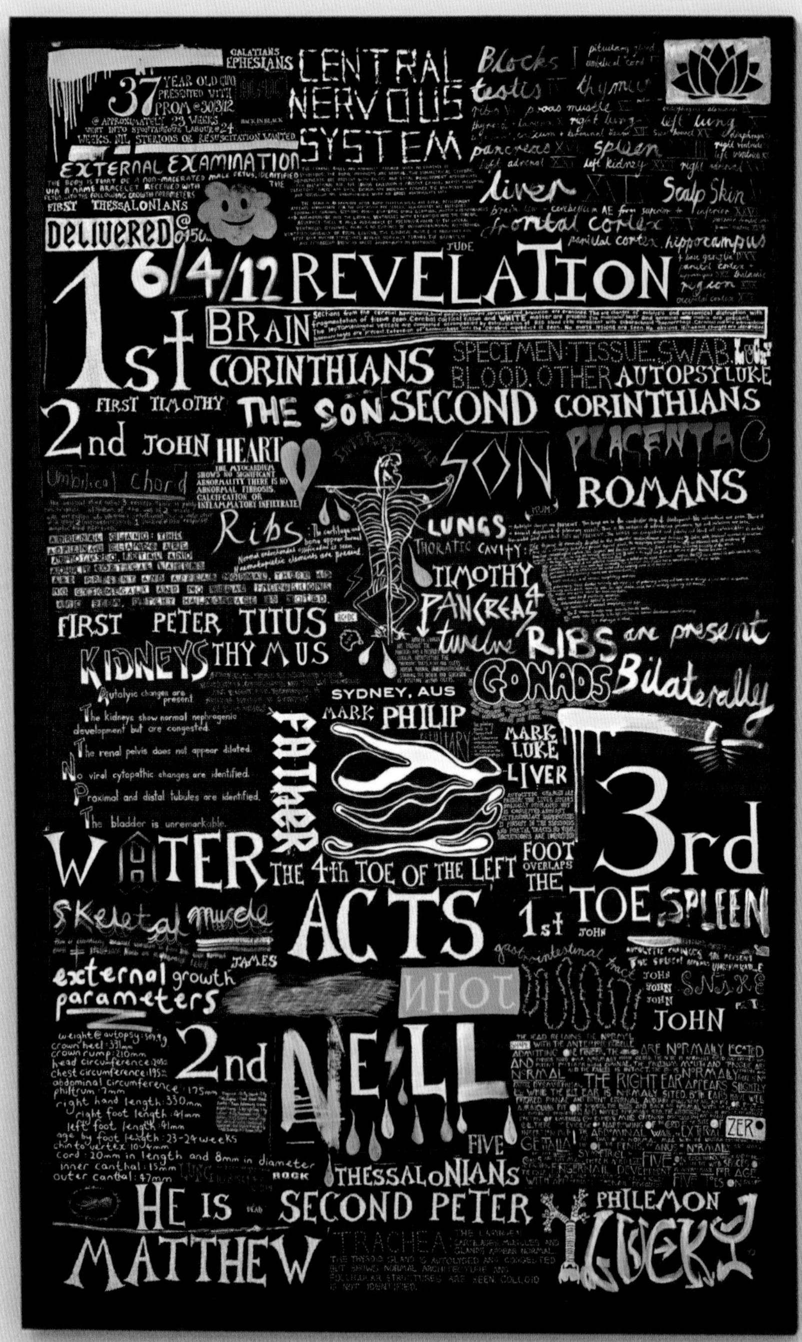

THE FIRSTBORN IS DEAD
2015

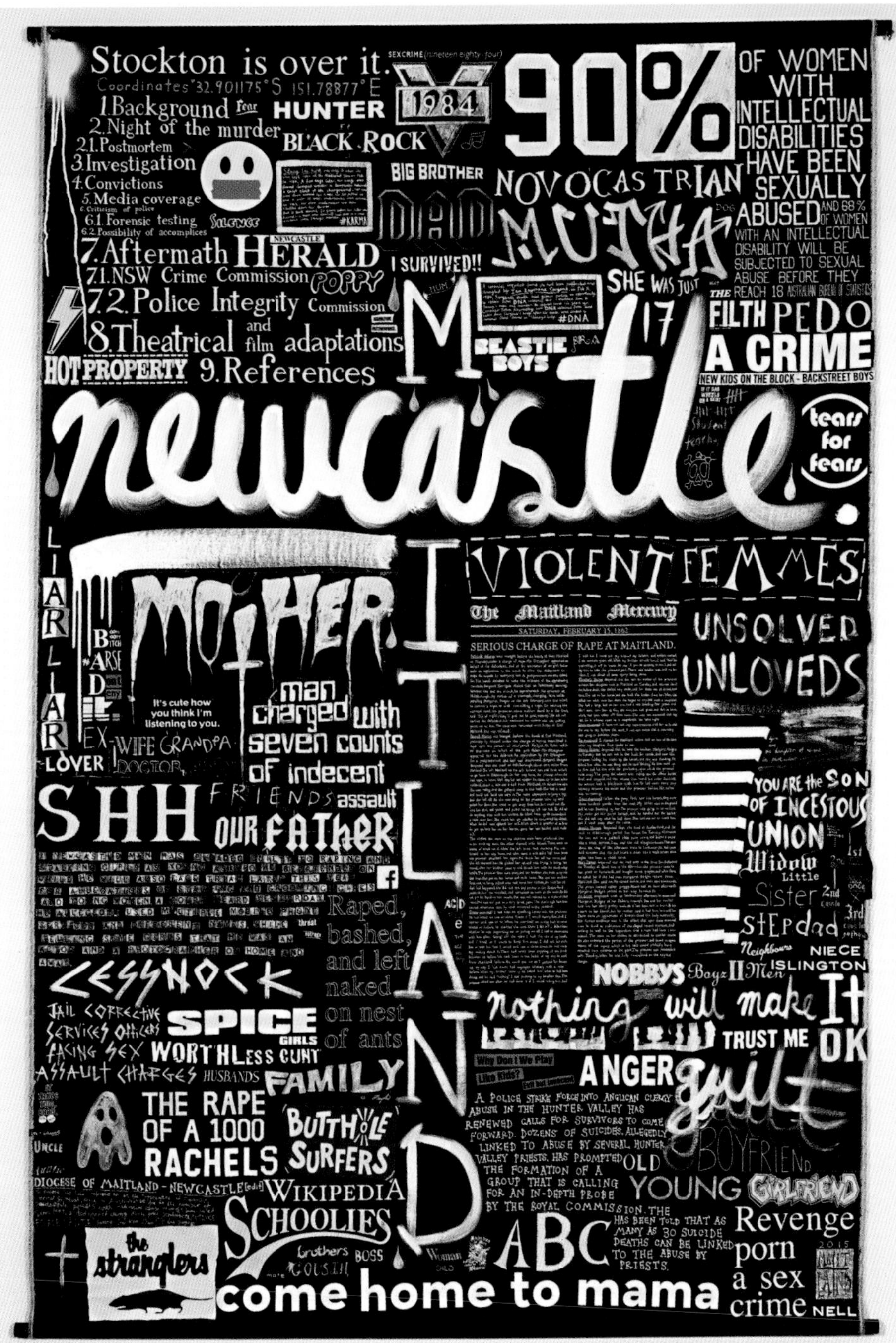

Where Newcastle meets Maitland
2015

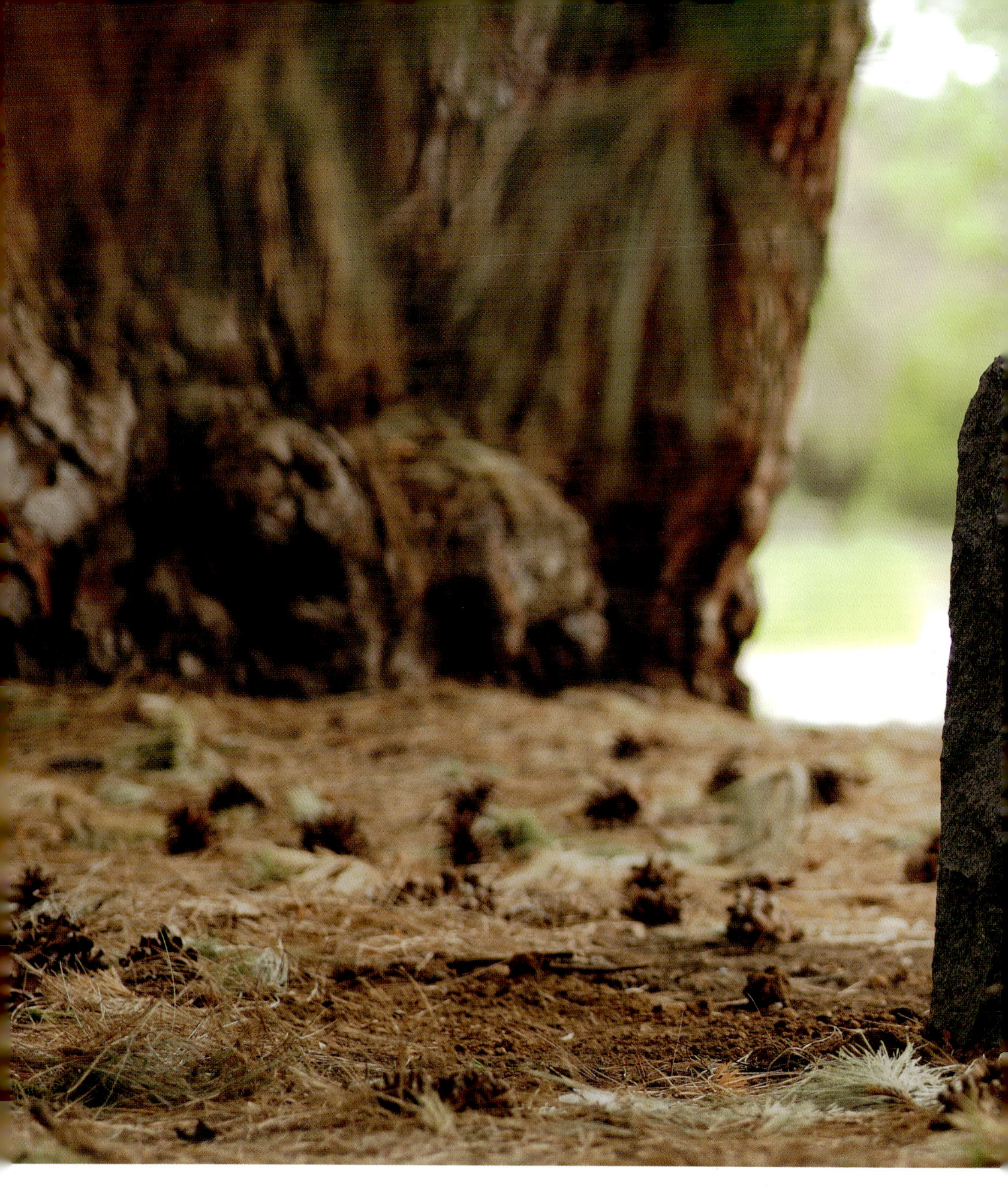

Happy Ending
2006

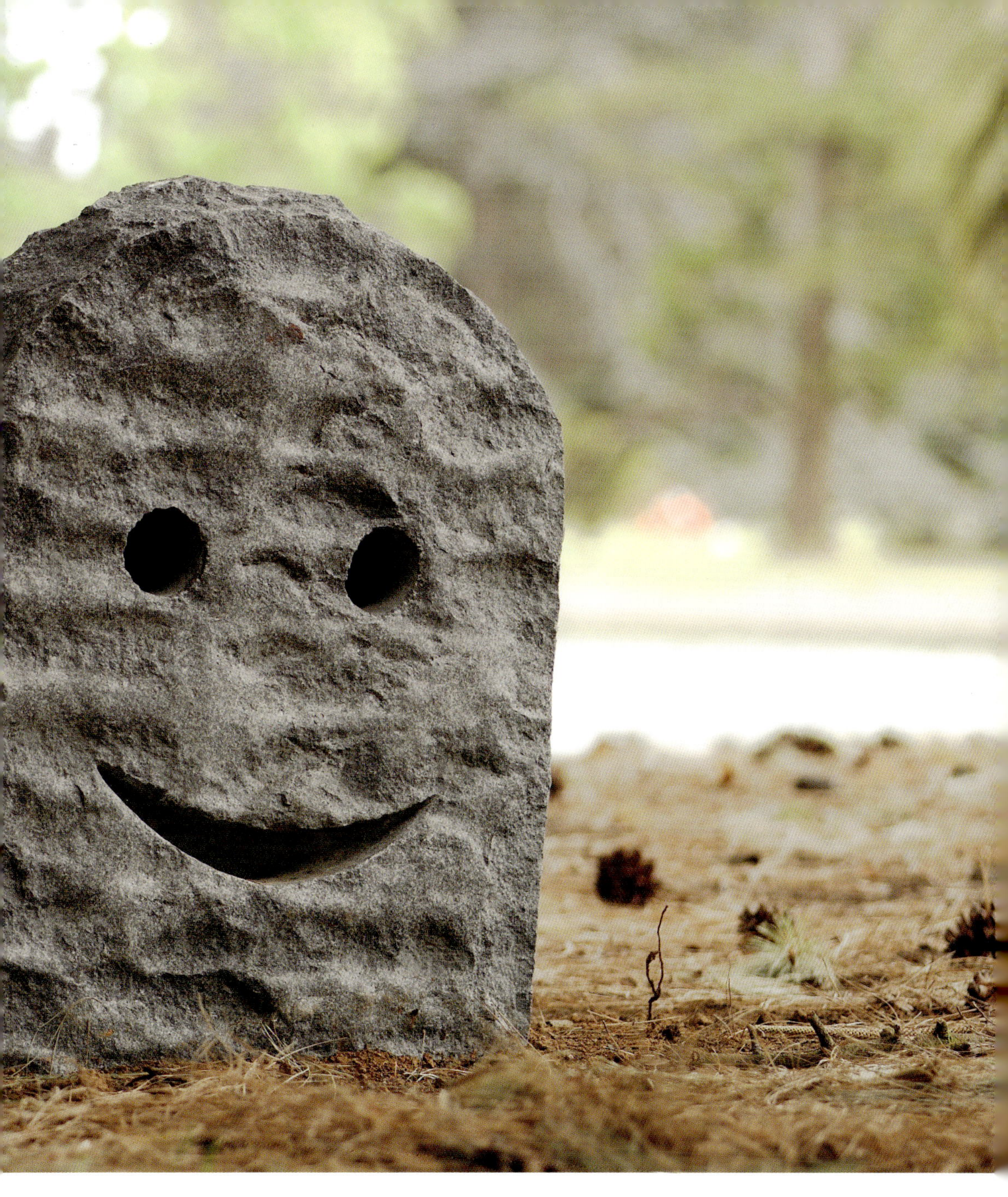

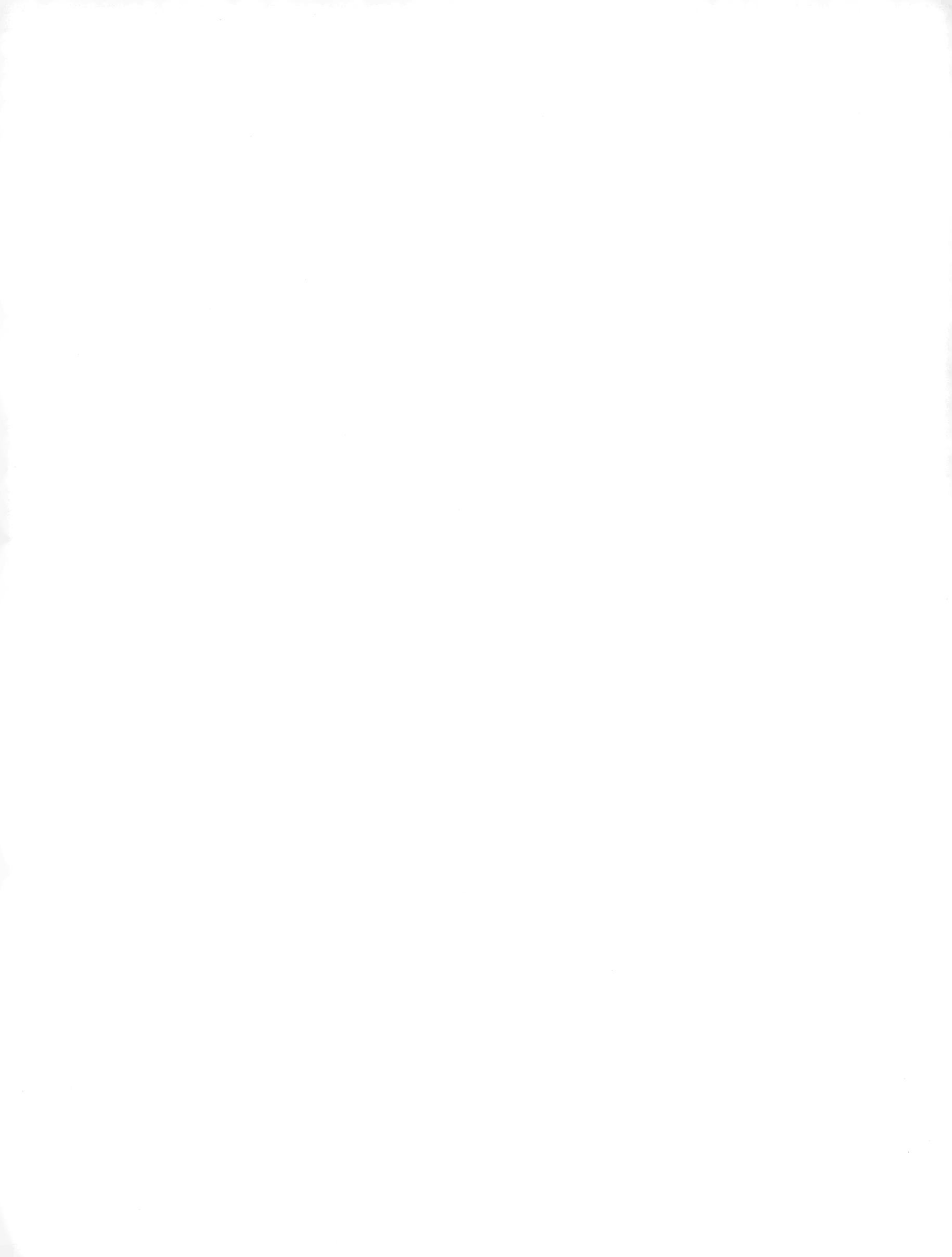

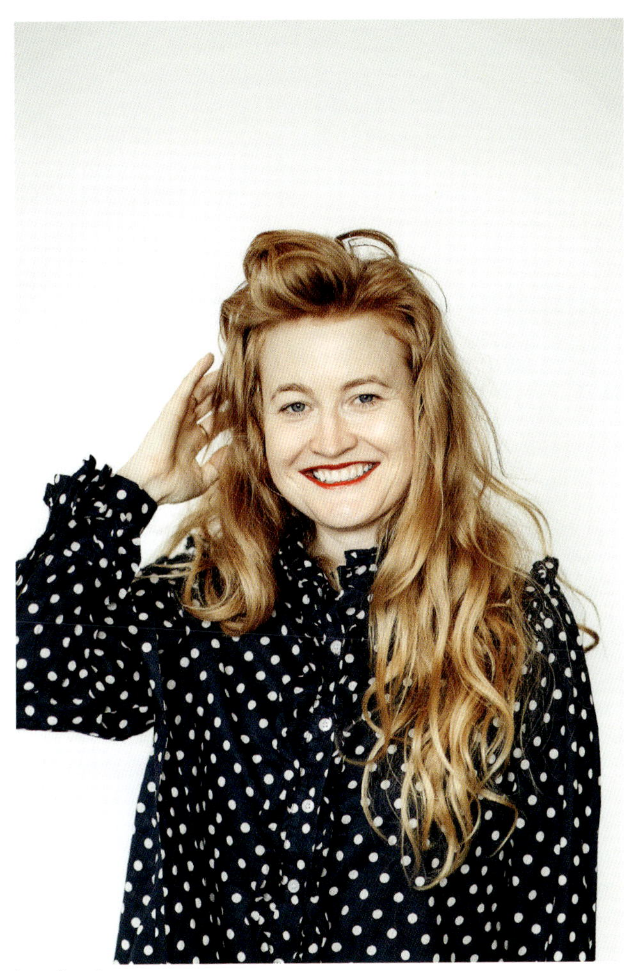

Image: Penny Lane

ARTIST

Nell is a Sydney-based artist with a practice that spans performance, installation, video, painting and sculpture. Born in Maitland, NSW, Nell studied under Lindy Lee at Sydney College of the Arts, the University of Sydney (1995); with Joan Jonas and John Baldessari at the University of California, Los Angeles (1996); and with Annette Messager at the École nationale supérieure des Beaux-Arts, Paris (2006). She has undertaken residencies at the British School at Rome; with Red Gate Gallery, Beijing; at the Australian National University, Canberra; and at Artspace, Sydney.

Nell's work has featured in more than 250 exhibitions worldwide, including *Primavera 1999*, Museum of Contemporary Art, Sydney; *Theatre of the World*, MONA, Hobart, and la maison rouge, Paris; and *Magic Object*, The Adelaide Biennial, Art Gallery of South Australia. Her solo exhibitions include *BLACK 'n' WHITE*, PS Project Space, Amsterdam; *NE/LL*, Shepparton Art Museum, Shepparton, VIC; and *Home Town Girl Has Wet Dream*, Maitland Regional Art Gallery, NSW. Nell won the University of Queensland National Artists' Self-Portrait Prize in 2013.

Instagram: @nellartist

ESSAYIST

Robert Forster is a Brisbane-based singer-songwriter, performer and author. His latest book is the memoir *Grant & I* (2016). His most recent album is *Inferno* (2019). In the late seventies, Forster co-founded the acclaimed rock band The Go-Betweens. In 2015, he was awarded an honorary Doctor of Letters by the University of Queensland.

SERIES EDITOR

Natalie King is an Australian curator, editor and arts leader with extensive expertise in international contemporary art. She is an Enterprise Professor at the Victorian College of the Arts, University of Melbourne.

She is curating Yuki Kihara's presentation for Aotearoa New Zealand, 59th Venice Biennale 2021. In 2020, she is curating an exhibition for the Tokyo Photographic Art Museum as part of the cultural programme of the Olympic Games.

In 2017, King was curator of *Tracey Moffatt: My Horizon*, Australian Pavilion at the 57th Venice Biennale, accompanied by a publication that she edited with Thames & Hudson.

She is widely published in arts media and is the current president of AICA-Australia (International Association of Art Critics). She was a finalist in the AFR 100 Women of Influence 2018.

CREDITS

8–9 *Unlimited Radiance*, 2001
Sequins, pins, acrylic on cork, mounted on MDF
381.6 x 409.6 cm
Courtesy of the artist and Roslyn Oxley9 Gallery, Sydney
Photo: Alex Davies
Collection: Museum of Contemporary Art, Sydney. Gift of Dr Edward Jackson AM and Mrs Cynthia Jackson AM, 2006

10 *ooh*, 2016
Cardboard, mica, resin, PVA, wool, wooden stool
2 parts: 84.4 x 27.4 x 21.5 cm (overall)
Courtesy of the artist and STATION, Melbourne
Photo: Jack Willet

11 *Who Made Who/One on One*, 2004–13
Gold leaf, acrylic, varnishes,
epoxy resin, wooden stool
71 x 25.2 x 22.2 cm
Courtesy of the artist and STATION, Melbourne
Photo: Jack Willet
Private Collection, Wellington, New Zealand

13 *the WORLD fleeting*, 2018
Acrylic on canvas
102 x 79.8 cm
Courtesy of the artist and Roslyn Oxley9 Gallery, Sydney
Photo: Luis Power

14 *Not just an Australian Problem*, 2018
Acrylic and mixed media on canvas
102.2 x 80.4 cm
Courtesy of the artist and Roslyn Oxley9 Gallery, Sydney
Photo: Luis Power
Collection: University of Queensland, Brisbane

15 *2020 NELL*, 2018
Acrylic on linen
103.5 x 81 cm
Courtesy of the artist and Roslyn Oxley9 Gallery, Sydney
Photo: Luis Power
Private Collection, Sydney

17 *Don't You See?*, 2018
Acrylic and mixed media on canvas
100.5 x 80.1 cm
Courtesy of the artist and Roslyn Oxley9 Gallery, Sydney
Photo: Luis Power
Collection: University of Queensland, Brisbane

18 *I AM just A SIMPLE ARTIST TRYING TO make MY WAY IN THE Universe*, 2018
Acrylic and mixed media on canvas
101.5 x 83.5 cm
Courtesy of the artist and Roslyn Oxley9 Gallery, Sydney
Photo: Luis Power
Collection: University of Queensland, Brisbane

19 *And KUNST Loves Me*, 2018
Acrylic on canvas
98.9 x 81.5 cm
Courtesy of the artist and Roslyn Oxley9 Gallery, Sydney
Photo: Luis Power
Private Collection, Sydney

20–1 *Blessings*, 2017–18
Acrylic, ink, mixed media and glitter on canvas or linen
12 paintings (from a series of 40)
Dimensions variable
Installation view: *Workshop*, University of Queensland Art Museum, Brisbane (3 June 2019 – 29 February 2020)
Courtesy of the artist and Roslyn Oxley9 Gallery, Sydney
Photo: Carl Warner
Collection: University of Queensland, Brisbane

23 *a white bird flies in the mist, a black bird flies in the night, a woman walks, wild and free, she is not afraid to die*, 2008
Bronze, mother-of-pearl, resin, hand-blown glass
Dimensions variable
Installation view: *There Goes a Narwhal*, Gertrude Contemporary, Melbourne (8 February – 8 March 2008)
Courtesy of the artist and Roslyn Oxley9 Gallery, Sydney
Photo: Mark Ashkanasy

25 *Mother and Child #2*, 2017
Hand-blown glass, metal stool
3 parts: 91.8 x 39.4 x 38.1 cm (overall)
Courtesy of the artist and STATION, Melbourne
Photo: Jenni Carter

26–7 *The Wake*, 2014–16
Stoneware, earthenware, concrete, bronze, glass, glaze, underglaze, polyurethane, varnish, acrylic, enamel, spray paint, fabric paint, pigment, oxide, BondCrete, decals, silver leaf, gold leaf, copper, glitter, wood, branches, dried flowers, natural and synthetic feathers, raffia pompom, *The Financial Times*, gold-plated aluminium, stainless steel, epoxy resin, foam, canvas, rubber, leather, wire, Vietnamese straw hat, newspaper, silver duct tape, ribbon, wool, cotton, buckwheat, crocodile skin, cobwebs, natural pearls, metal and wooden stools
Dimensions variable
Installation view: *Magic Object*, The 2016 Adelaide Biennial of Australian Art, Art Gallery of South Australia, Adelaide (27 February – 15 May 2016)
Courtesy of the artist, Roslyn Oxley9 Gallery, Sydney, and STATION, Melbourne
Photo: Saul Steed
Collection: Art Gallery of South Australia, Adelaide

28 *History is Now*, 2014–15
Stoneware, glaze, enamel, wooden stool
3 parts: 57.2 x 20.2 x 33.4 cm (overall)
Courtesy of the artist and Roslyn Oxley9 Gallery, Sydney
Photo: Jenni Carter
Collection: Art Gallery of South Australia, Adelaide

29 *3 words and good BYE*, 2015–16
Stoneware, underglaze, wooden stool
2 parts: 132.8 x 38.8 x 41.5 cm (overall)
Courtesy of the artist and Roslyn Oxley9 Gallery, Sydney
Photo: Jenni Carter
Collection: Art Gallery of South Australia, Adelaide

31 *dark DEAtH*, 2015
Earthenware, underglaze, wooden stool
2 parts: 110 x 33.3 x 32.5 cm (overall)
Courtesy of the artist and Roslyn Oxley9 Gallery, Sydney
Photo: Jenni Carter
Collection: Art Gallery of South Australia, Adelaide

33 *THE END*, 2014–15
Stoneware, acrylic, polyurethane, wood
2 parts: 63 x 29 x 28.5 cm (overall)
Courtesy of the artist and Roslyn Oxley9 Gallery, Sydney
Photo: Jenni Carter
Collection: Art Gallery of South Australia, Adelaide

35 *Mother of the Dry Tree*, 2017
Acrylic and mixed media on linen, wood
296.5 x 223 cm
Courtesy of the artist and Roslyn Oxley9 Gallery, Sydney
Photo: Jenni Carter

36 *1, 2, 3, 4, 5, 6, 7, 8, nell (washed away)*, 2010
Enamel on New Zealand kiln-dried pine
213 x 76 cm
Courtesy of the artist and Roslyn Oxley9 Gallery, Sydney
Photo: Ivan Buljan

singing from the same hymn book – the songs the Lord taught us, 2010
Enamel on New Zealand kiln-dried pine
2 parts: 202.6 x 75.8 cm (overall)
Courtesy of the artist and Roslyn Oxley9 Gallery, Sydney
Photo: Ivan Buljan

37 *from mother to daughter – all relationships are endless*, 2010
Enamel on New Zealand kiln-dried pine
2 parts: 214.6 x 76 cm (overall)
Courtesy of the artist and Roslyn Oxley9 Gallery, Sydney
Photo: Ivan Buljan

one happy cloud – many raindrips, 2010
Enamel on New Zealand kiln-dried pine
202.6 x 75.8 cm
Courtesy of the artist and Roslyn Oxley9 Gallery, Sydney
Photo: Ivan Buljan
Private Collection, Byron Bay

39 *Made in the Light – Happy Cloud and Drips*, 2011
Neon
Dimensions variable
Installation view: Maitland Regional Art Gallery, NSW, 2019
Commissioned by Allens, Sydney, 2011
Courtesy of the artist and Roslyn Oxley9 Gallery, Sydney
Photo: Clare Hodgins
Collection: Maitland Regional Art Gallery, NSW

41 *The Ghost Who Walks will Never Die*, 2005
Acrylic on canvas
91.3 x 65.9 cm
Courtesy of the artist and Roslyn Oxley9 Gallery, Sydney
Photo: Greg Weight
Private Collection, Sydney

43 *Who Made Who*, 2004
Gold leaf, acrylic and enamel, varnish, epoxy resin, foam
36.5 x 25 x 25 cm
Courtesy of the artist and Roslyn Oxley9 Gallery, Sydney
Photo: Adrian Cook
Collection of Julian and Stephanie Grose, Adelaide

45 *The Dr. said it was like being hit by lightning*, 2013
Neon
156 x 112 cm
Edition of 5 + AP 2
Courtesy of the artist and Roslyn Oxley9 Gallery, Sydney
Photo: Jessica Maurer
Collection: University of Queensland Art Museum, Brisbane, and Private Collection, Adelaide

47 *Let R.I.P*, 2013
Vinyl records, cardboard record sleeve, stainless steel
44 x 30 x 30 cm
Courtesy of the artist and STATION, Melbourne
Photo: Jack Willet
Private Collection, Melbourne

48 *the gateless, pearly gate*, 2010
Natural pearls, enamel, epoxy resin, foam
64.5 x 44 x 44 cm
Courtesy of the artist and Roslyn Oxley9 Gallery, Sydney
Photo: Adrian Cook
Collection of Julian and Stephanie Grose, Adelaide

50–1 *self-nature is subtle and mysterious – nun.sex.monk. rock*, 2010
Fibreglass, silver leaf, varnish, nickel-plated bronze
2 parts: 91 x 75 x 59 cm (Nell size); 121 x 8 x 4 cm (stick size)
Courtesy of the artist and Roslyn Oxley9 Gallery, Sydney
Photo: Adrian Cook

52 *More Sound Hours Than Can Ever Be Repaid – Back in Black, #4, 1980/2013*, 2013
Cardboard record sleeves
219.5 x 220.4 cm
Courtesy of the artist and STATION, Melbourne
Photo: Jack Willet

53 *More Sound Hours Than Can Ever Be Repaid – The White Album, #1, 1968/2013*, 2013
Cardboard record sleeves
251.5 x 253.5 cm
Courtesy of the artist and Roslyn Oxley9 Gallery, Sydney
Photo: Jessica Maurer
Private Collection, Sydney

54–5 *Not Without My Tail*, 2004
Crocodile tail, enamel, epoxy resin, gold leaf, card, varnish
2 parts: 11 x 15 x 97 cm (overall)
Courtesy of the artist and Roslyn Oxley9 Gallery, Sydney
Photo: Adrian Cook

56–7 *Let Me Put My Love Into You*, 2006
Wool, cotton
161 x 300 cm
Courtesy of the artist and Roslyn Oxley9 Gallery, Sydney
Commissioned by Deutsche Bank, Sydney
Weavers: Sue Batten, John Dicks, Pamela Joyce (Australian Tapestry Workshop)
Photo: Jenni Carter
Collection: Deutsche Bank, Sydney

58 *The Perfect Drip*, 1999
Enamel on fibreglass, polyurethane foam, wood, polyvinyl chloride pipe, filler, primer
237 x 150 cm
Installation view: *Primavera*, Museum of Contemporary Art, Sydney (8 September – 29 November 1999)
Courtesy of the artist and Roslyn Oxley9 Gallery, Sydney
Image courtesy: National Gallery of Australia, Canberra
Private Collection, Perth

61 *if you could hear the sound of my violin you would know how I feel*, 2015
Wood
2 parts: 60.4 x 20.6 x 7.5 cm (object 1); 60.5 x 20.7 x 8.3 cm (object 2)
Courtesy of the artist and STATION, Melbourne
Photo: Jenni Carter

62–3 *Let There Be Robe*, 2012
Zen robe, T-shirts, beads, badges, mannequin, socks, Converse All Star sneakers, guitar picks, paintbrushes, drumsticks, scissors, pencils, screwdrivers, chopsticks
Dimensions variable
Installation view: Roslyn Oxley9 Gallery, Sydney (26 November – 18 December 2015)
Commissioned by MONA, Hobart, 2012
Courtesy of the artist and Roslyn Oxley9 Gallery, Sydney
Photos: Jessica Maurer (62); Penny Lane (63)
Collection: Home of the Arts, Gold Coast

64–5 *When BLACK turns GOLD 1980/2013*, 2013
Acrylic, gold leaf and varnishes on paper, cardboard record sleeve
47.1 x 78.6 cm
Courtesy of the artist and STATION, Melbourne
Photo: Jessica Maurer

66 *Sgt. Happy 1967/2014*, 2014
Mixed media on cardboard record sleeve
46 x 46 cm
Courtesy of the artist and STATION, Melbourne
Photo: Jack Willet
Private Collection, Melbourne

67 *HAPPY DAY'S NIGHT 1964/2015*, 2015
Mixed media on cardboard record sleeve
46 x 46 cm
Courtesy of the artist and STATION, Melbourne
Photo: Jack Willet
Private Collection, Melbourne

68–9 *QUIET/LOUD* (still), with Bec Machine from Baby Machine, 2012
Single-channel digital video; 16:9, colour
Edition of 5 + AP 2
Commissioned by Campbelltown Arts Centre for *Transmission* (9 June – 5 August 2012)
Courtesy of the artist and Roslyn Oxley9 Gallery, Sydney
Videography: Tina Havelock Stevens
Sound: Ingrid Rowell
Photo: Zan Wimberley
Collection: University of Queensland Art Museum, Brisbane

70–1 *THE Labyrinth*, 2015
3-day performance
Installation view: Carriageworks, Sydney
Commissioned by Performance Space for Day for Night (20–22 February 2015)
Courtesy of Roslyn Oxley9 Gallery, Sydney, and STATION, Melbourne
Photo: Alex Davies
Edited by Boccalatte

72–3 *The Six Strings That Drew Blood*, 2012
Guitar strings, glass, crystal
4 x 23 x 23 cm
Courtesy of the artist and Roslyn Oxley9 Gallery, Sydney
Photo: Jessica Maurer

74–5 *Apples and Oranges*, 2007
Bronze
Apple and orange size
Edition of 5 + AP 2
Courtesy of the artist and Roslyn Oxley9 Gallery, Sydney
Photo: Adrian Cook
Private Collections, Melbourne and Sydney

76 *empty vessel*, 2015
Mirror-polished bronze, dead blowfly
7.5 x 10.5 cm
Edition of 5 + AP 2
Courtesy of the artist and STATION, Melbourne
Photo: Jenni Carter

78–9 *SUMMER* (stills), 2012
Single-channel digital video; 16:9, colour
Edition of 5 + AP 2
Courtesy of the artist and Roslyn Oxley9 Gallery, Sydney
Videography: Tina Havelock Stevens
Sound: Ingrid Rowell
Collection: University of Queensland Art Museum, Brisbane, and Private Collection, Sydney

80–1 *Where there are humans, you'll find flies, 1949/2013*, 2013
Book, stickers
55 x 73 cm
Courtesy of the artist and Roslyn Oxley9 Gallery, Sydney
Photo: Jessica Maurer
Collection: Maitland Regional Art Gallery, NSW

82–3 *A Short History of Rock 'n' Roll – My Grey Album #1, 1968/2013*, 2013
Acrylic on cardboard record sleeves
47.6 x 78.8 cm
Courtesy of the artist and Roslyn Oxley9 Gallery, Sydney
Photo: Jessica Maurer

84–5 *THE FIRSTBORN IS DEAD* (detail), 2015
Acrylic, pencil and mixed media on linen
217 x 129 cm
Courtesy of the artist and STATION, Melbourne
Photo: Jenni Carter
Collection of Rae-ann Sinclair and Nigel Williams, Lake Hawea, New Zealand

86 *THE FIRSTBORN IS DEAD*, 2015
Acrylic, pencil and mixed media on linen
217 x 129 cm
Courtesy of the artist and STATION, Melbourne
Photo: Jenni Carter
Collection of Rae-ann Sinclair and Nigel Williams, Lake Hawea, New Zealand

87 *Where Newcastle meets Maitland*, 2015
Acrylic, pencil and mixed media on linen, wood
224 x 154 cm
Commissioned by The Lock-Up, Newcastle, for *Exhibit A* (30 October – 6 December 2015)
Courtesy of the artist and Roslyn Oxley9 Gallery, Sydney
Photo: Jenni Carter
Collection: Art Gallery of New South Wales, Sydney

88–9 *Happy Ending*, 2006
Noble black granite
20 x 70 x 90 cm
Installation view: Werribee Park, Victoria (1 March – 27 May 2007)
Courtesy of the artist and Roslyn Oxley9 Gallery, Sydney
Photo: Ross Bird
Collection: University of Queensland Art Museum, Brisbane, and National Gallery of Victoria, Melbourne

First published in Australia in 2020
by Thames & Hudson Australia Pty Ltd
11 Central Boulevard, Portside Business Park
Port Melbourne, Victoria 3207
ABN: 72 004 751 964

www.thamesandhudson.com.au

23 22 21 20 5 4 3 2 1

Thames & Hudson Australia wishes to acknowledge that Aboriginal and Torres Strait Islander people are the first storytellers of this nation and the traditional custodians of the land on which we live and work. We acknowledge their continuing culture and pay respect to Elders past, present and future.

978 1 7607607 4 8

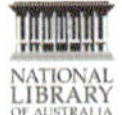

A catalogue record for this book is available from the National Library of Australia

Every effort has been made to trace accurate ownership of copyrighted text and visual materials used in this book. Errors or omissions will be corrected in subsequent editions, provided notification is sent to the publisher.

Front cover:
Lightning Bolt, 2013
Neon, 50 x 17 cm
Edition of 5 + AP 2
Courtesy of the artist and Roslyn Oxley9 Gallery, Sydney
Photo: Jessica Maurer

Design: Evi-O.Studio | Evi O & Rosie Whelan
Series editor: Natalie King
Printed and bound in China by 1010

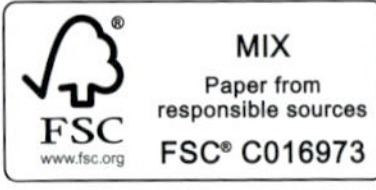

FSC® is dedicated to the promotion of responsible forest management worldwide. This book is made of material from FSC®-certified forests and other controlled sources.

Other artists in this series

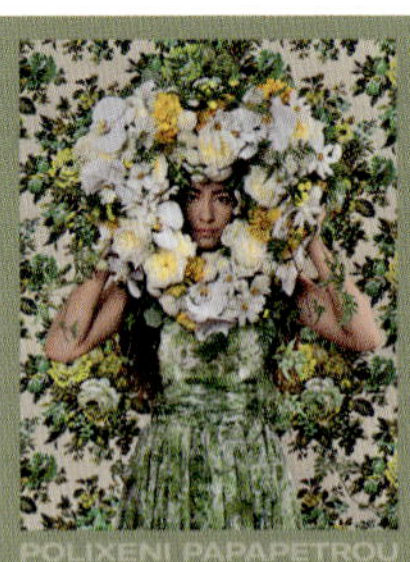

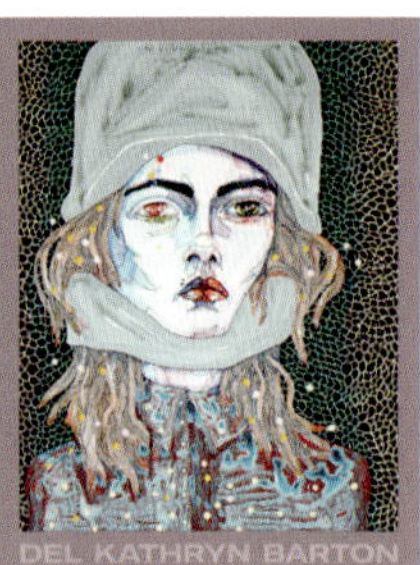

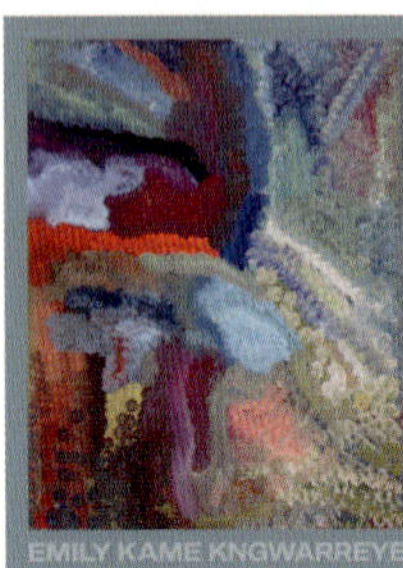